'My Maasai' is an initiative of Jan Hoek, in collaboration with Kenyan based photographers; Sarah Waiswa (uganda), Mohamed Altoum (Sudan), Joel Lukhovi (Kenya) as well as students of the De-Capture Limited school of photography.

How the Maasai
are always photographed

oogle maasai  

Alle Afbeeldingen Video's Maps Nieuws Meer Instellingen Tools

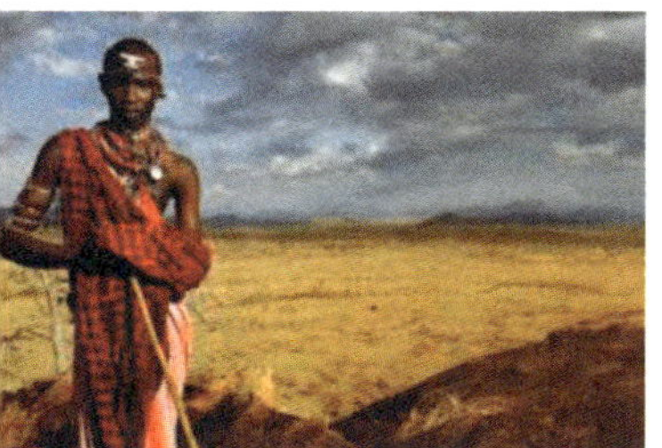
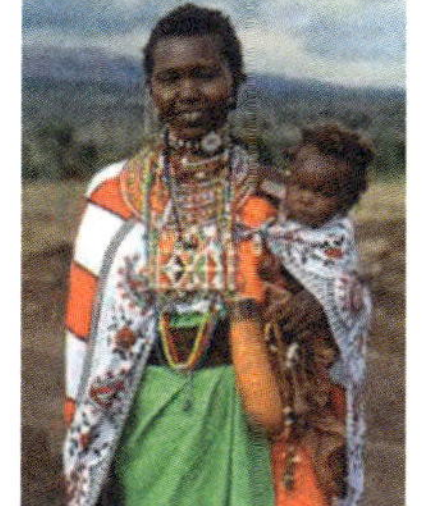
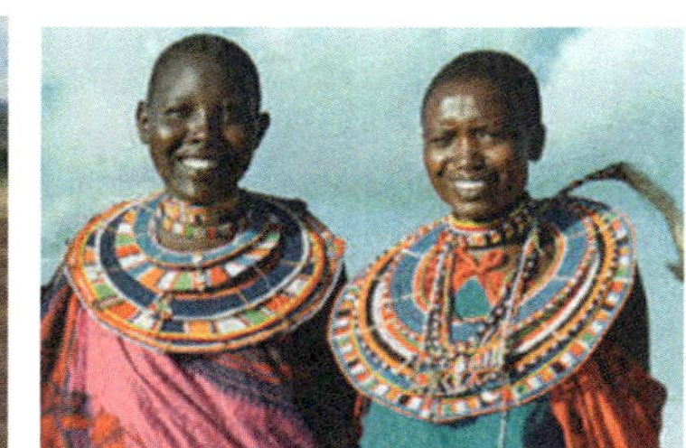
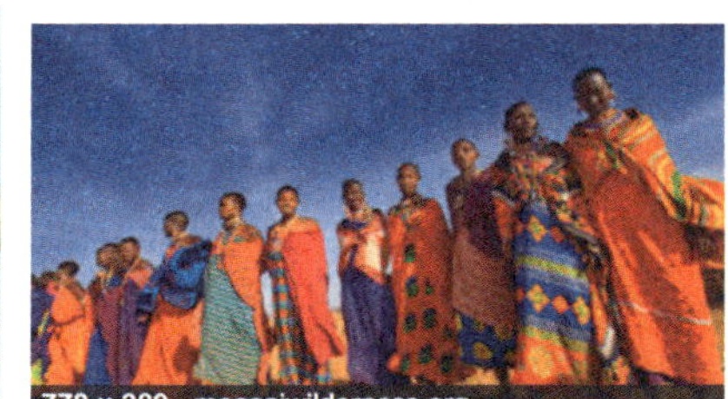
778 × 389 - maasaiwilderness.org
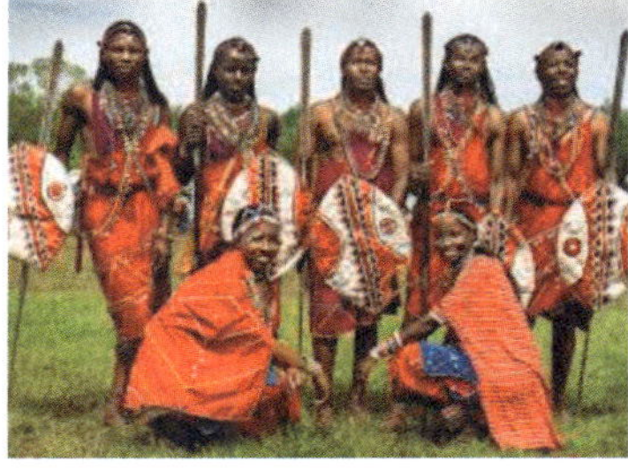
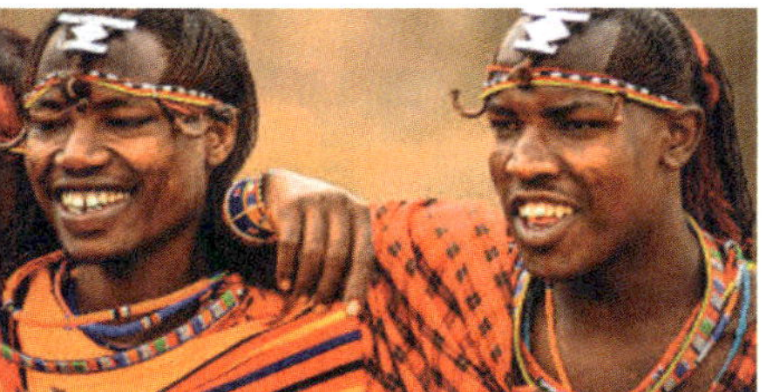
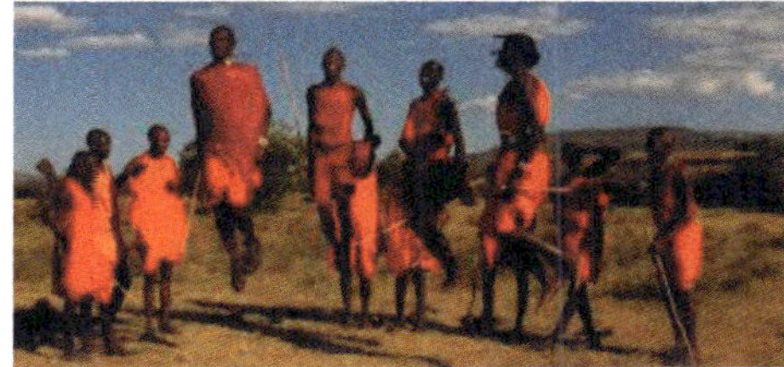
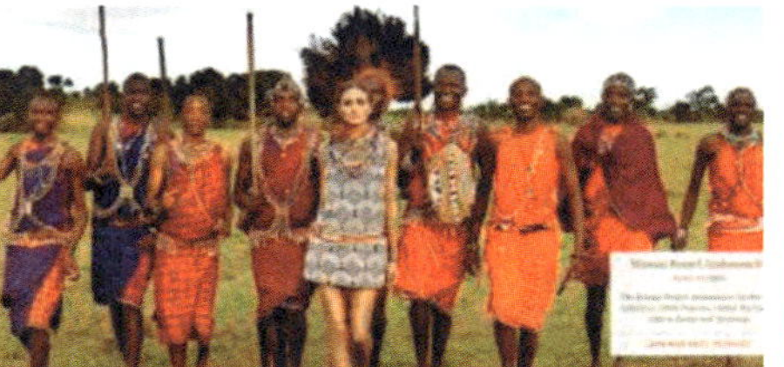
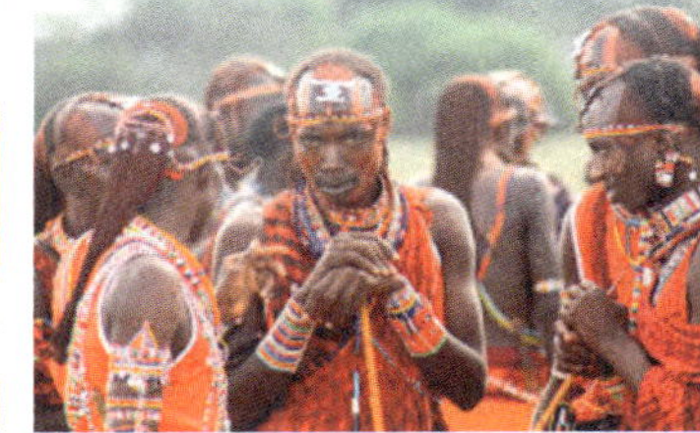
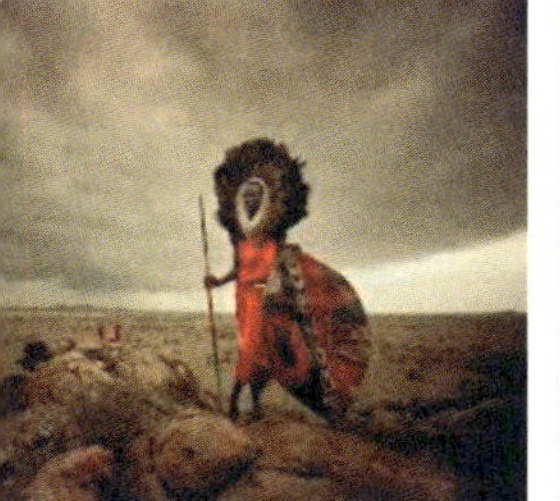
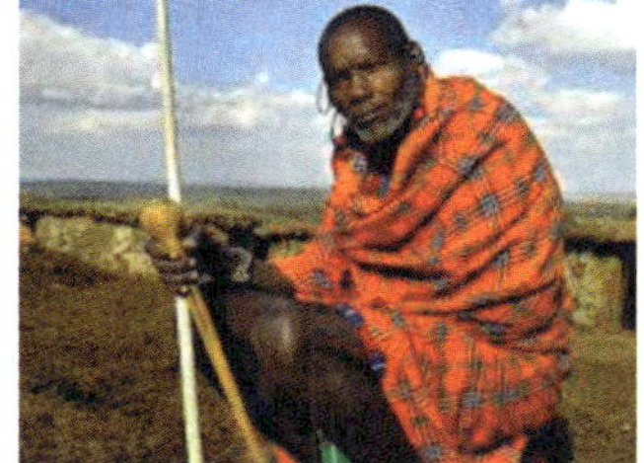
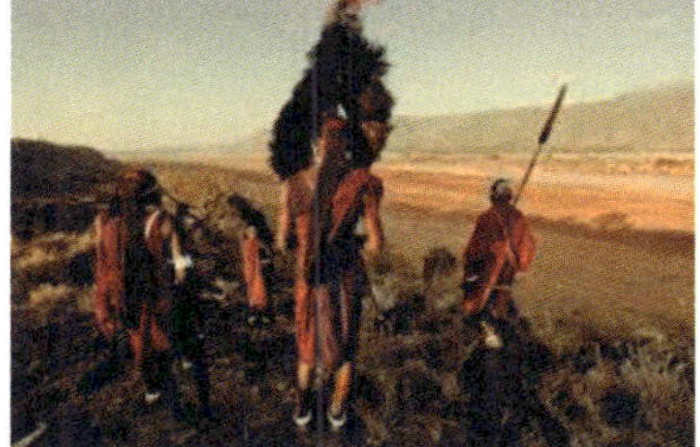
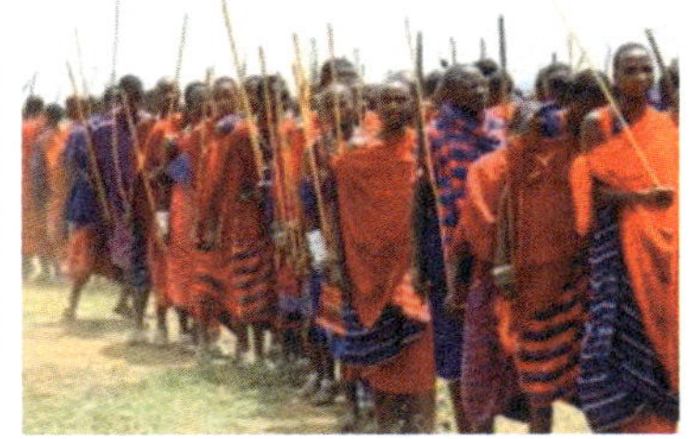
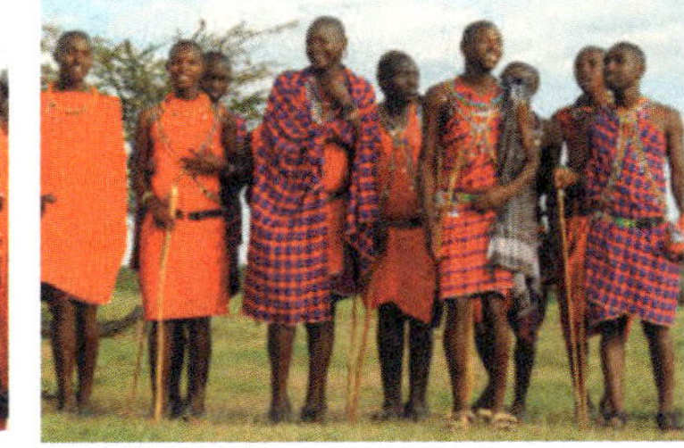
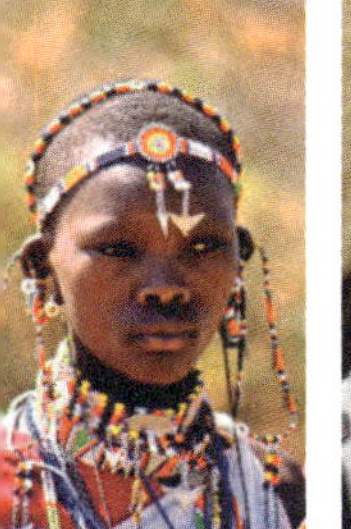
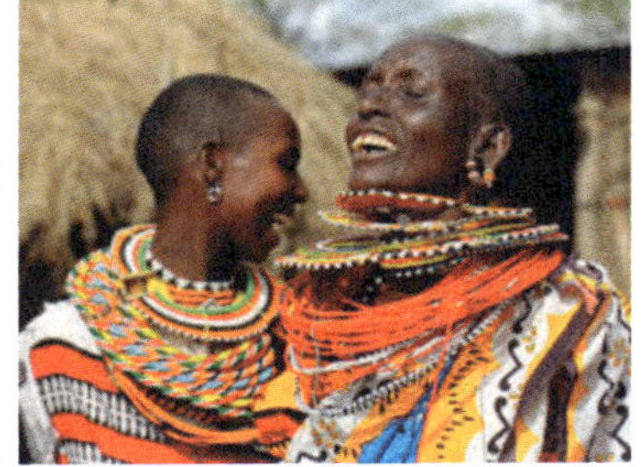
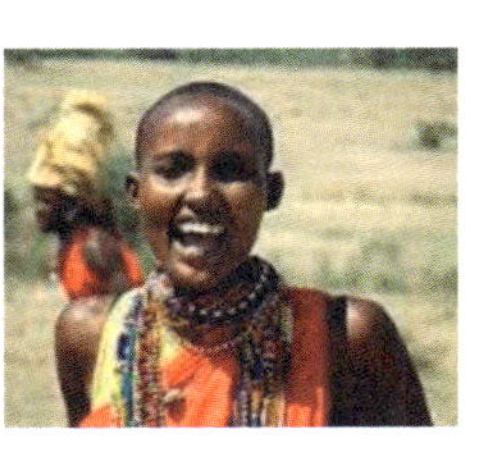
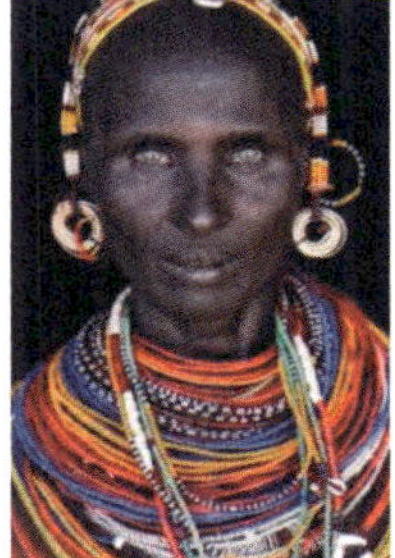
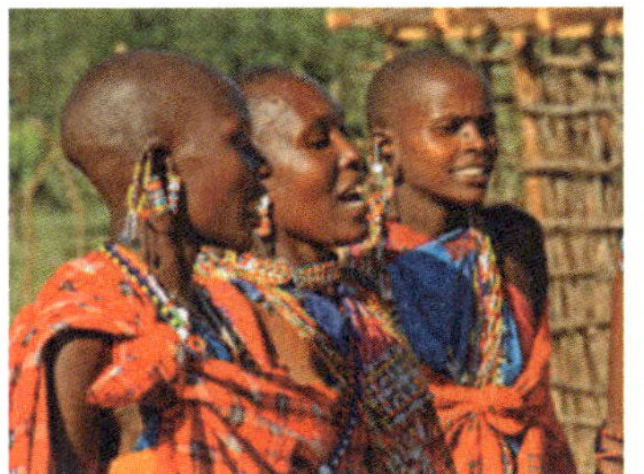
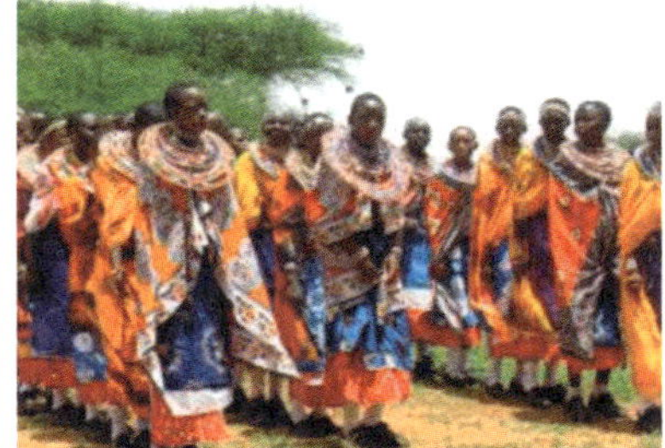
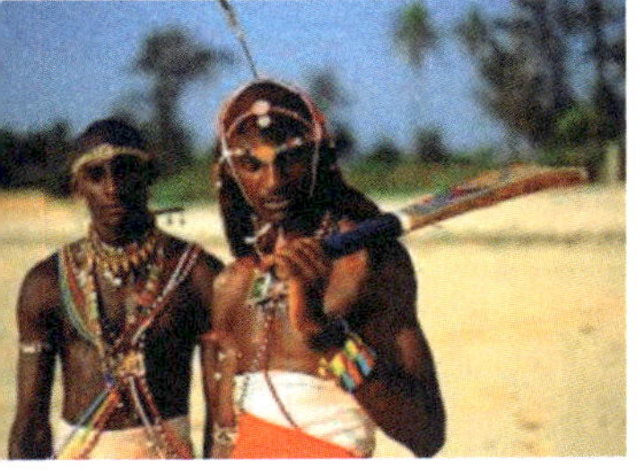
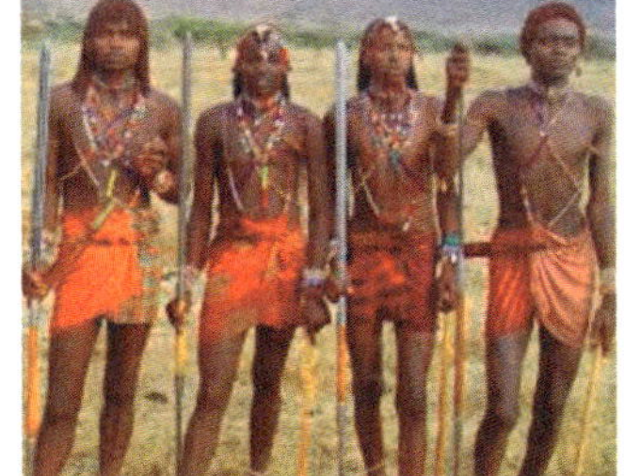
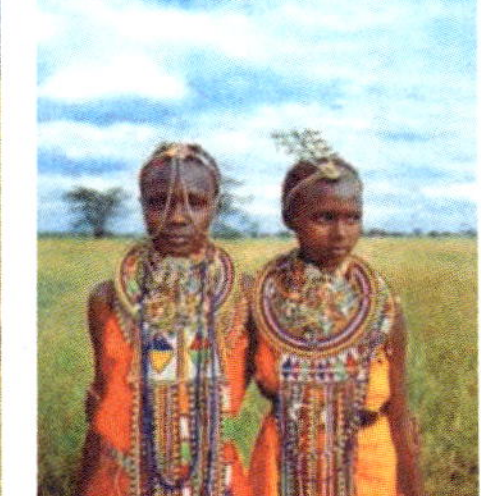
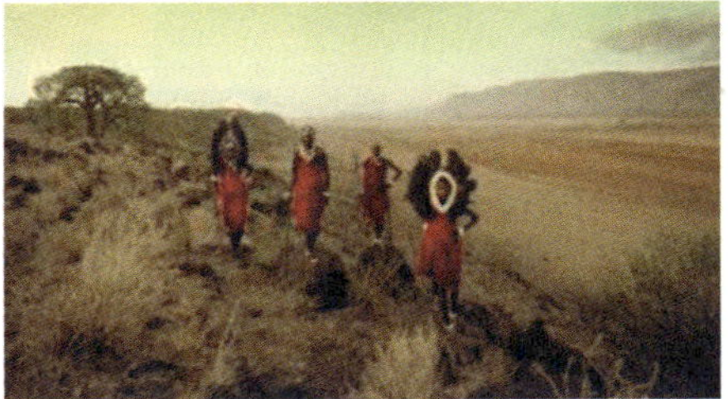
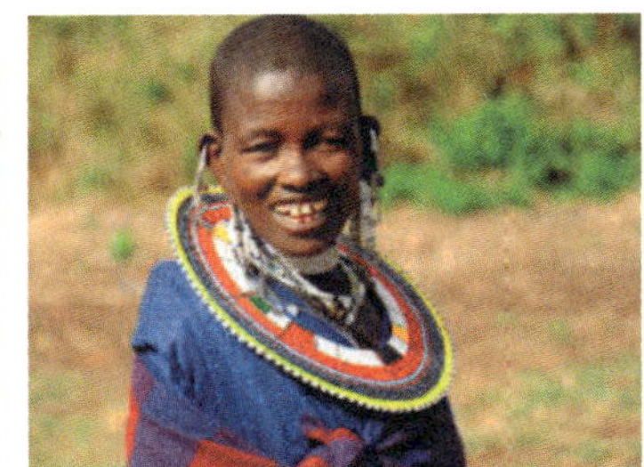
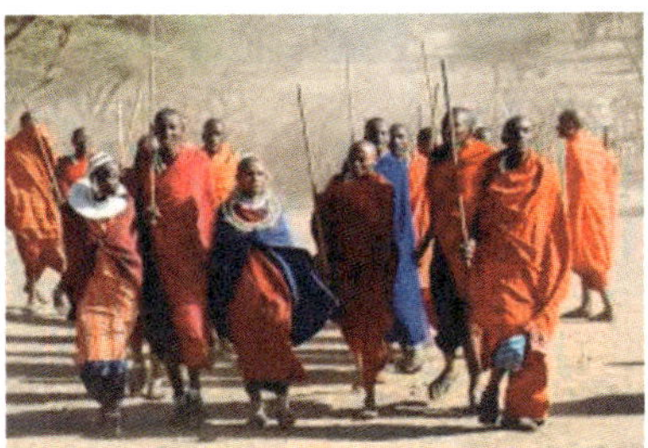
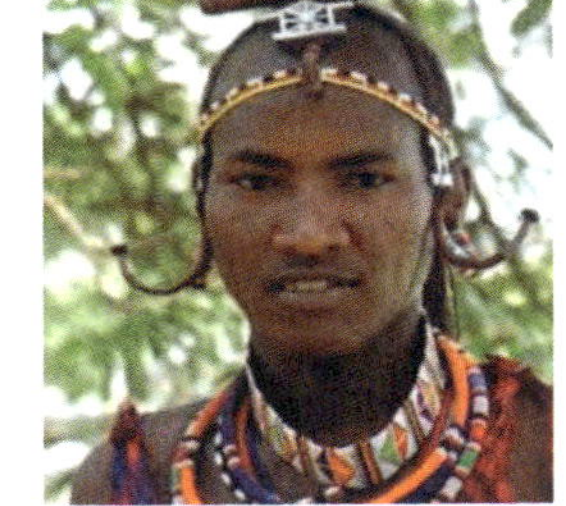
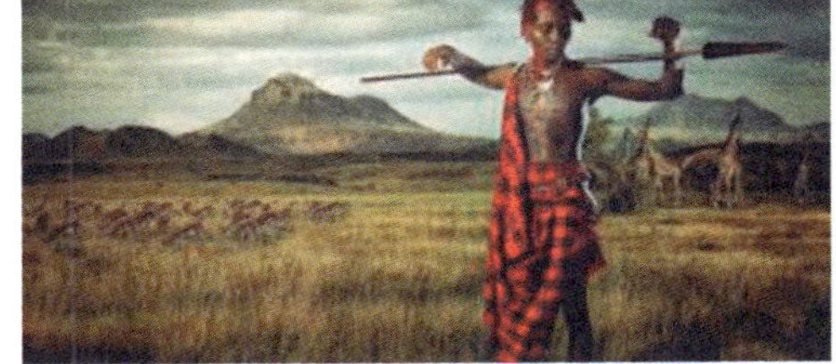
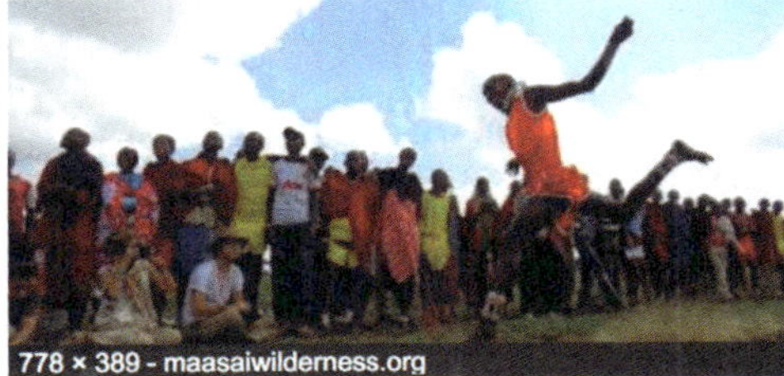
778 × 389 - maasaiwilderness.org
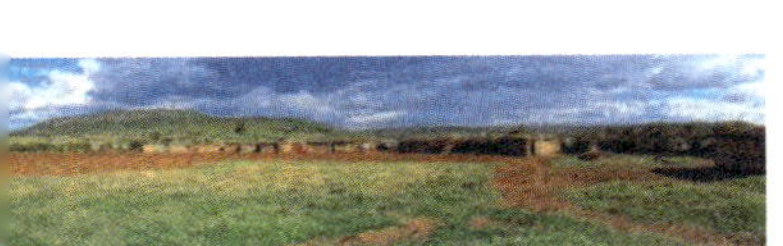
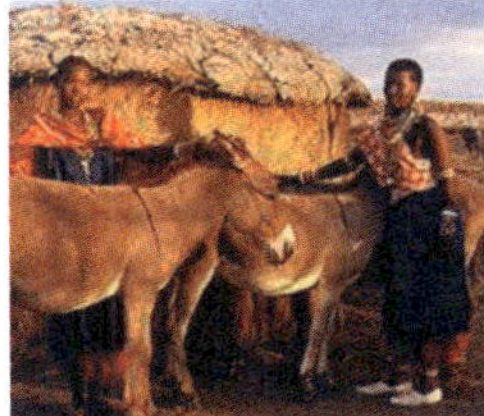
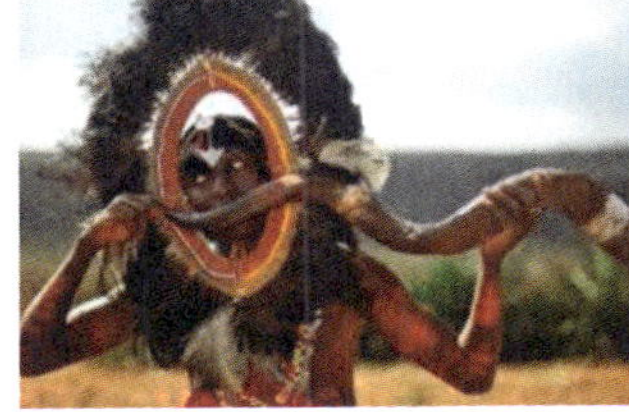
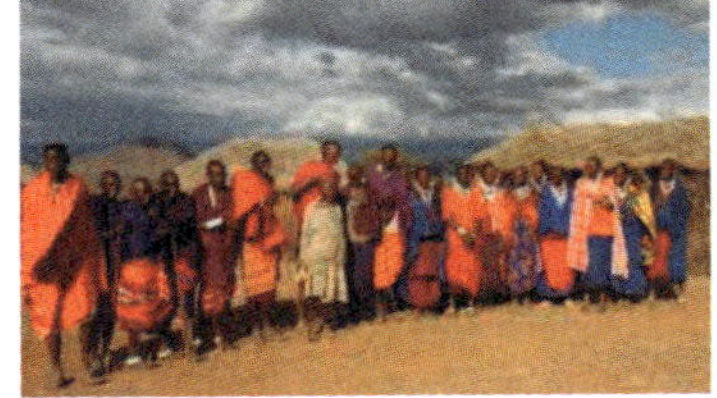
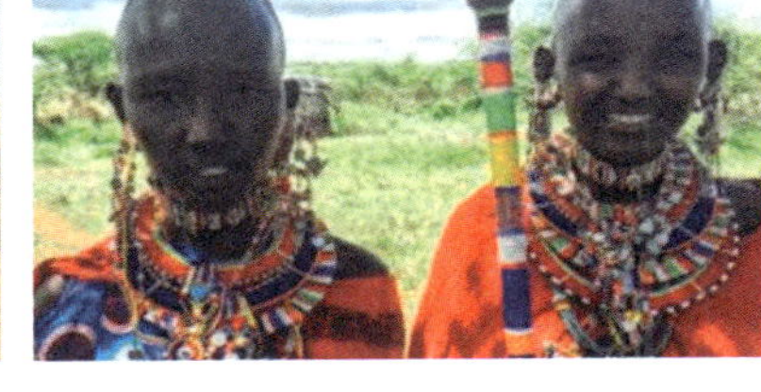
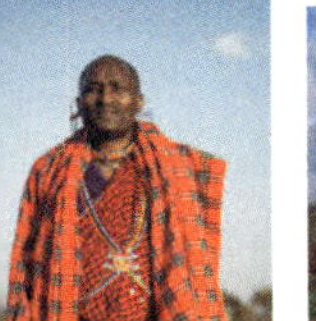
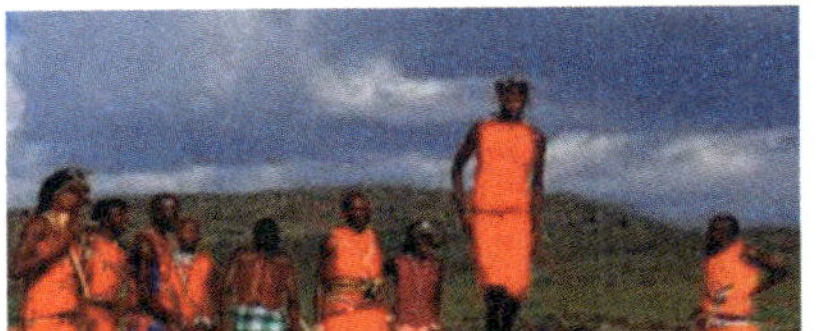
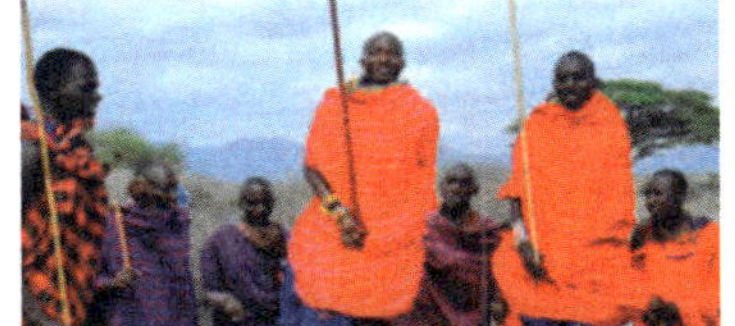
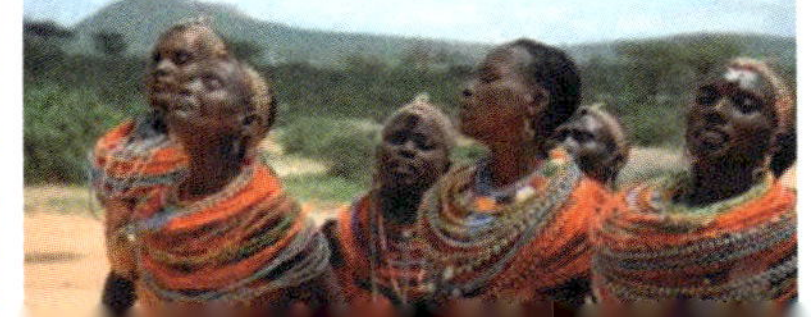
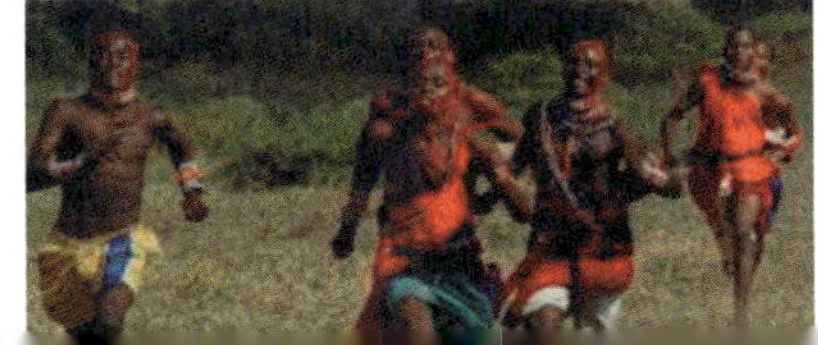

introduction

The Maasai are the most photographed people from the East African region, and perhaps even, greater Africa. However, most of the images of the Maasai which the world has come to know and love are composed and captured by far removed Western photographers whose narrow representations of this diverse tribal group are almost always manifested in jumping warriors and bare chested women struggling to look past a swarm of flies into the camera lens while balancing snotty faced tots on their hips.

Time has come for the people of this wonderful land to reconstruct this narrative and show through their own images, how they see the modern Maasai. Yes, the Maasai still jump with the astonishing capability they are widely celebrated for and yes they still adorn themselves with swathes of beautiful traditional fabrics and ornate beadwork, but like any other society, the Maasai have evolved into a more complex multidimensional community to keep up abreast of the times.

The Maasai people being among the last in the region who still display a strong, visual cultural identity find themselves at that inevitable intersection where modernity with all its trappings faces off with the ethnocultural. It is a crucial moment in the history of their kind. One that must be recorded truthfully and fairly for the world today and for posterity 'My Maasai' is a brave and socially significant project bringing together photographers from different backgrounds across Eastern Africa to convey their personal mental impressions of the Maasai people today.

text credits: Koranja Nzisa

With thanks to Siji Jabbar for editorial advice
and English translation.

Jan Hoek

Preface

I've had to think long and hard about whether to write a preface for this book. My Maasai is meant to portray the Maasai from an East African perspective, and as such should contain little that might distract attention from the subject. Furthermore, there are lots of Kenyans and Tanzanians, such as Karanja Nzisa, who can write about the subject much more insightfully than I possibly could. Nonetheless, I instigated this project, and my role is likely to raise questions; thus, it would be odd, not to mention deceitful, to erase any trace of my involvement. With that in mind, the following is my attempt to explain my role in this project.

A few years ago, I published a book called New Ways of Photographing the New Masai. (I was unaware at the time that only Westerners spell it 'Masai', rather than 'Maasai', as the locals do, and as I have since done.) I had already lived in Tanzania for a few years when I got the idea for the book. I've never been a big fan of nature, so I'd been based in the capital city, Dar es Salaam. During my time there, I encountered lots of Maasai people (a tribe of which I had been hitherto completely unaware) going about their day, and they looked so cool to me that I quickly developed something of an obsession with them. I was struck, among other things, by the seemingly casual way in which they combined the traditional red chequered cloth (the shuka) with the latest Nike trainers, by the way some stowed their mobile phone by having it dangle from a stretched earlobe, and by the Maasai businessmen sporting white facial markings.

But when I got back to the Netherlands, I searched in vain for a single photograph of a Maasai person that captured what I had seen. All the photographs I found were interchangeable, and portrayed the Maasai as homogeneous groups leaping in place against a rural backdrop. An internet search quickly yielded what was clearly everyone's favourite, generic Maasai shot: a selfie of a sunburnt white tourist with an arm flung around the shoulders of a traditionally dressed Maasai man.

The photographs also had another thing in common: the complete absence (or omission) of any trace of modernity (unless a Westerner was in the frame). I returned to Tanzania with the idea of putting together a book about city dwelling Maasai, but portrayed as no one appeared to have previously considered. This was not to deny the existence of Maasai who conformed to the common portrayal, nor to forbid anyone from photographing the Maasai in this manner. I merely believed that this generic portrayal represented a limited view of reality.

To avoid the limitations of my own perspective, I decided to collaborate with a handful of Arusha-based Maasai 'models', and portray them as they would wish to be portrayed. I knew that if I took

Jan Hoek

Preface

just one shot of each model, I would run the risk of offering a less than adequate interpretation of their wishes. So I shot three interpretations each. They would still be my interpretations, but the models would at least have a choice of images from which to determine which of these came closest to what they had in mind, which they considered the next best interpretation, and, equally important, which they considered an outright failure. I included all three in the book, with captions identifying each shot's ranking according to the respective model. And whenever I exhibited the photographs, I always made sure their preferred choice was the largest print on display, and their least favourite image the smallest. I included the 'failures', both in the book and in the exhibitions, because how a person prefers not to be portrayed reveals something about their self-image, too.

The models saw and 'approved' all images for publication, and were paid for their time. Some uploaded their preferred image to Facebook to serve as their profile picture, and my relationship with some of them grew into friendship. I'm an not the most technically proficient photographer in the world, and as a result my work can occasionally appear somewhat less than polished, as though shot by a child. I was prepared for the odd comment about this, but I didn't anticipate any other form of criticism, and certainly not with respect to any ethical failings on my part. Who, after all, would object to a book that set out to combat stereotypes and gave its models a say in how they were depicted?

At first, the book met with critical acclaim. 'At long last, the cliché-ridden portrayal of the Maasai bites the dust!' was a typical response. I was invited to exhibit my work, and my book appeared in bookstores from Tokyo all the way to New York (which sounds more impressive than it actually was, since we're talking about a print run of just 1,000 copies).

Coincidentally, another book about the Maasai —and a hugely popular one it would prove to be— hit the stores at about the same time. This one, by the British photographer Jimmy Nelson, and titled Before They Pass Away, romanticised the Maasai yet again as some sort of exotic and unspoiled, indistinguishable human specimen. This, along with a Valentino ad campaign featuring leaping Maasai as a backdrop, revealed how little had changed in the way the West has portrayed the Maasai since the colonial era and Leni Riefenstahl's famous shots from the 1950s.

The positive reception was, however, soon followed by some less than positive criticism, including a broadside in Aperture, arguably the most influential photography journal in the world. In an essay titled 'The Lives of Others', the photographer and writer Stanley Wolukau-Wanambwa took apart my book. Stanley argued that much as I might

Jan Hoek

Preface

like to believe that I had handed over control of the portrayal of the Maasai to the models themselves, it was quite clear who held the reins in the relationship. He also felt that while I could claim with some legitimacy to have done something commendable by portraying the Maasai in a new and cliché-free manner, the fact that I, as a white Westerner, was determining the parameters within which African tribes such as the Maasai were to be portrayed (and, by default, within which the models made their choices), it was yet another example of how regrettably little had actually changed. In other words, the power to determine how Africans are seen remained in the West.

My initial response was defensive. 'Must I, from now on, excuse myself from working as a photographer in Africa simply because I'm a white Westerner?' I wondered. 'Must the continent be ring-fenced to ensure that non-African photographers are free to work anywhere in the world but Africa.' To address this issue publicly, I published a piece titled 'The (Im)possibilities to Shoot as a White Photographer on the African Continent' on American Suburb X, an online platform dedicated to photography. Here I advocated a playing field that accommodated everyone, African and Western photographers alike, and expressed my utopian vision of a future in which curiosity about 'the other', with full acknowledgement of the past, is considered a virtue, and in which this curiosity creates a multiplicity of projects that depict the world and its inhabitants in as many ways as possible. In this vision, photographers from all corners of the world would have the freedom (and the financial means) to execute these projects. I still believe in this utopian vision expressed in the piece; but at the same time, I have had to acknowledge a growing awareness of my denial of my responsibility as a Western photographer operating on the African continent.

The more time passed, the more I found myself in agreement with the criticisms. I realised that while I could get away with maintaining my defensive stance about Western photographers being allowed the freedom to shoot wherever they please, my obstinacy would simply be helping to ensure that nothing changed in the balance of power concerning how Africa and Africans were portrayed.

My changing view on the matter was validated one day during lunch with some photographers in Nairobi, where I was working on another project. They were Sarah Waiswa, Mohammed Altoum and Joel Lukhovi. It turned out that Sarah and Mohammed had also been working on the subject of the Maasai in an urban environment. In my ignorance, it hadn't occurred to me until that moment that not only was I not the first to be struck by the idea, but that it had probably

Jan Hoek

Preface

occurred to East African photographers long before it had to anyone else. All I'd done that they hadn't was publish a book about it and assume I was the first person to ever photograph the Maasai as part of the modern world.

I was also promptly informed of another faux pas that I had unwittingly committed. I claimed in my previous book to have collaborated with the Maasai models, yet while the book was available in London and Paris, it wasn't in Tanzania or Kenya, where the Maasai actually live. Consequently, I had contributed to restricting the debate to the West, and reduced the Maasai yet again to passive bystanders, or mere objects.

We thus decided to work together on a new book, only this time we would do things the right way. Among other things, it would be from an East African perspective, and made available in Kenya and Tanzania. We would temper the profit motive by raising the necessary funds through crowdfunding.

Sarah, Mohammed and Joel made it crystal clear that this was to be a partnership of equals, so I was not to approach this with the attitude of someone who imagined he was 'helping' them or doing them a favour. I wouldn't be the first Westerner to propose a collaborative venture, only to present it as a once-in-a-lifetime opportunity for an African photographer. The reality today is that most African photographers no longer need a thing from the West. For instance, Sarah, Mohammed and Joel all exhibit their work at photo festivals across thecontinent (and beyond), criss-cross the continent in execution of their independent projects, and could, if they so wished, afford to rely entirely on the economically thriving city of Nairobi for their livelihood.

As an outsider, once you start to get a sense of the degree of creative and entrepreneurial vibrancy that characterises the continent's photography scene, and begin to register its sheer wealth of talent, you can't help but wonder why most photography books, exhibitions and photojournalist reports about Africa published or held in the West feature the works of Western photographers exclusively.

In no way, therefore, is My Maasai about me 'helping' anyone. Rather, it is merely an attempt to make room for African photographers in so self-evident a manner that it could pass for the status quo.

That is why none of my own photographs appear in the book.

It then occurred to us that this project might be a useful way to showcase the work of young East African photographers. So we teamed up with the D-Capture School of Photography in Nairobi. The class included two Dutch students, a situation not altogether unusual given the city's cosmopolitan character, and after much discussion

Jan Hoek

Preface

we decided to include their work, too, as outsiders among insiders. Sarah proposed the title 'My Maasai' in reference to the idea that everyone in East Africa sees the Maasai through their own lens, and what they see is based on their personal experience of the individual Maasai they have met, on where they grew up and on the nature of their upbringing. The four of us were on hand to provide whatever guidance the students required, and made the final selection. We then mounted a huge outdoor exhibition of our selection opposite the Kenya National Archives building, a spot along which tens of thousands pass every day, thus exposing the work to as many people as possible for contemplation and discussion.

I realise that my role in the project remains a thorny issue: in an ideal world, a project such as this wouldn't involve someone like me at all. However, given the state of things, I also believe that as long as white photographers continue to be responsible for most of the photography projects executed in Africa for a Western audience, every white photographer benefitting from this imbalance has a responsibility to make room for African photographers, too. Because that space you're occupying is rightfully theirs. Which isn't to say that if you are one such photographer, you must now excuse yourself from working on the continent; merely that you should first do some research to see if 'your' idea isn't already being explored by an African photographer. It also means you should be prepared to collaborate with local photographers and artists, and even give up 'your' seat, so to speak, on occasion, or whenever an African colleague is available to carry out the assignment.

Above all, I believe that Western photographers such as myself need to train ourselves to become less sensitive and fragile, and accept that our position in this equation is quite rightly an issue. This means we must also accept the scrutiny of our approach to work, and of the work itself. We needn't be alarmed by this; no one ever died of constructive criticism. Rather, we must consider these criticisms carefully to see if they suggest ways to slowly modify our approach with the aim of creating a model that benefits everyone. This is not to suggest that the approach we adopted in putting together My Maasai is the ideal model of what I am advocating here. But I do hope it's a step in the right direction.

If nothing else, My Maasai shows that if twenty East African photographers take the Maasai as a subject, it will yield twenty completely different interpretations of the Maasai. And that is already twenty times richer than the single image of the leaping Maasai that Western photographers persist in propagating.

Mohamed Altoum

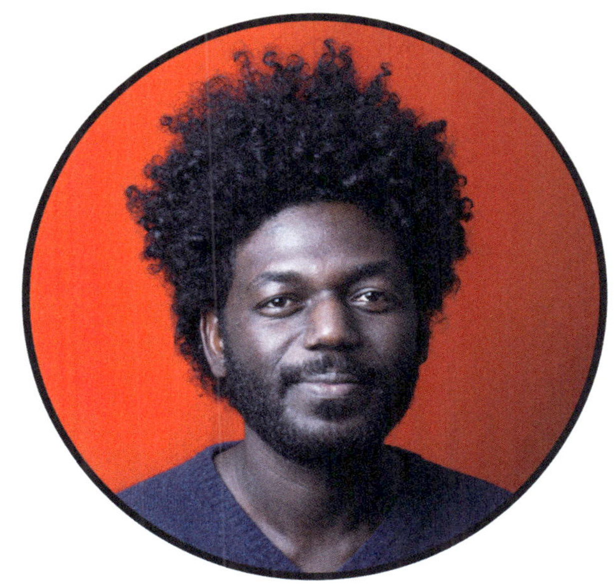

Grew up in: Khartoum, Sudan
Age: 33

Growing up and living in Khartoum, Nubian photographer Mohamed Altoum came in contact with people from the pastoralist ethnic groups of South Sudan whose customs are evocative of the Maasai way of life. He often wondered about the urban migrants who still identified strongly with a home they had left behind and how they reconciled the longing to return with a desire to find their feet in the big city. In 'My Maasai', Mohamed masterfully gives us a glimpse of this strife through the eyes of a Maa woman living in Nairobi.

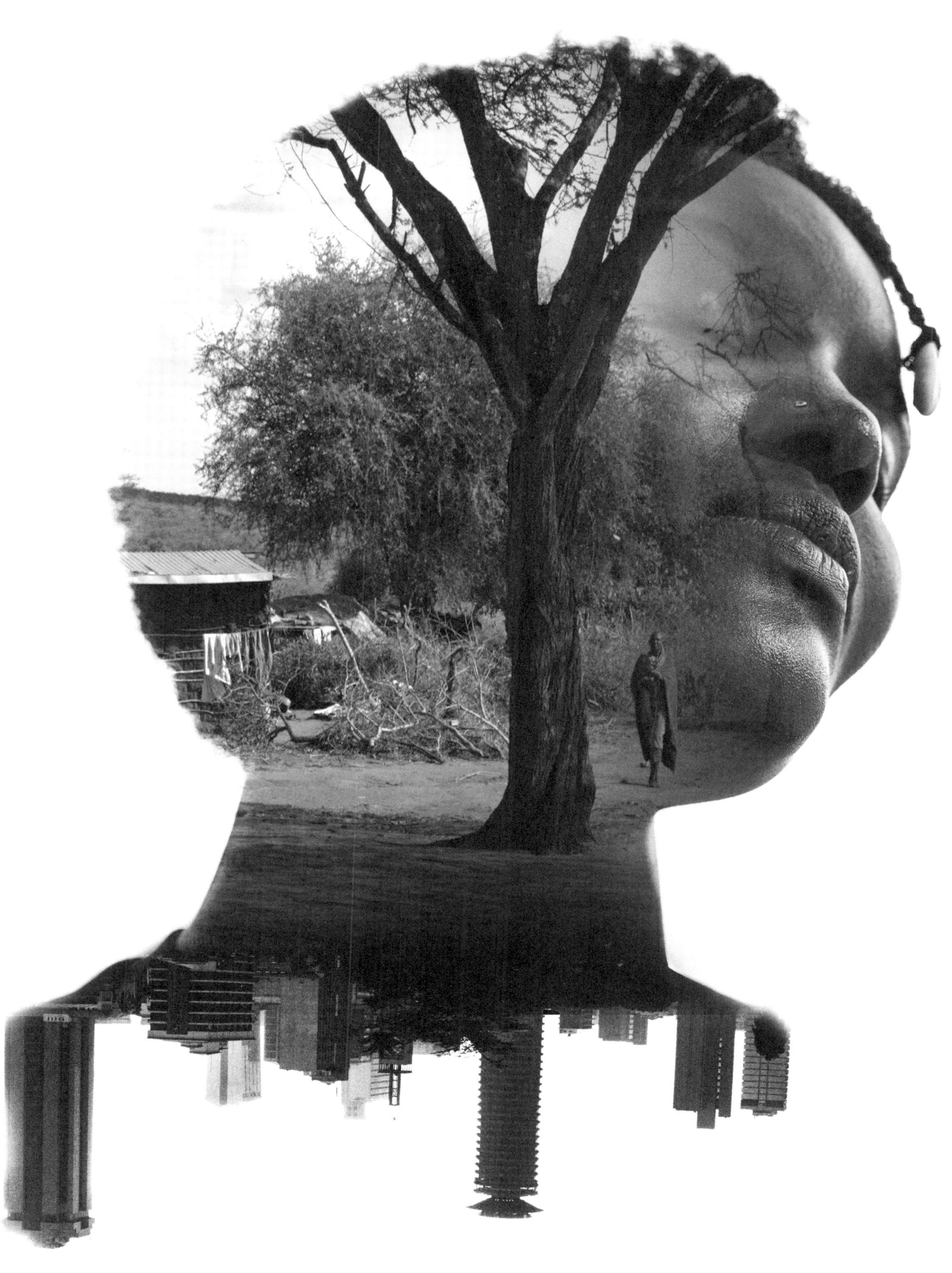

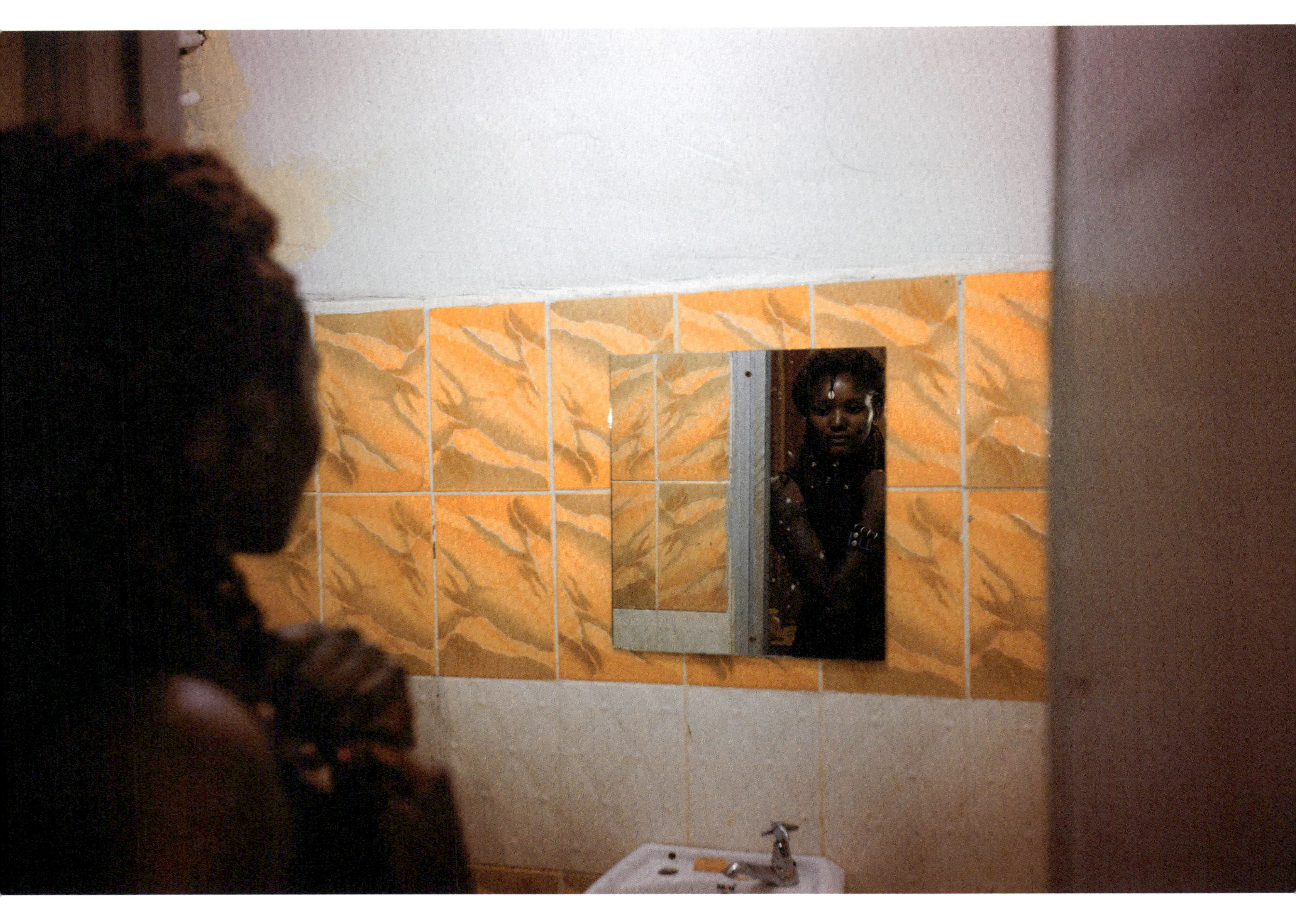

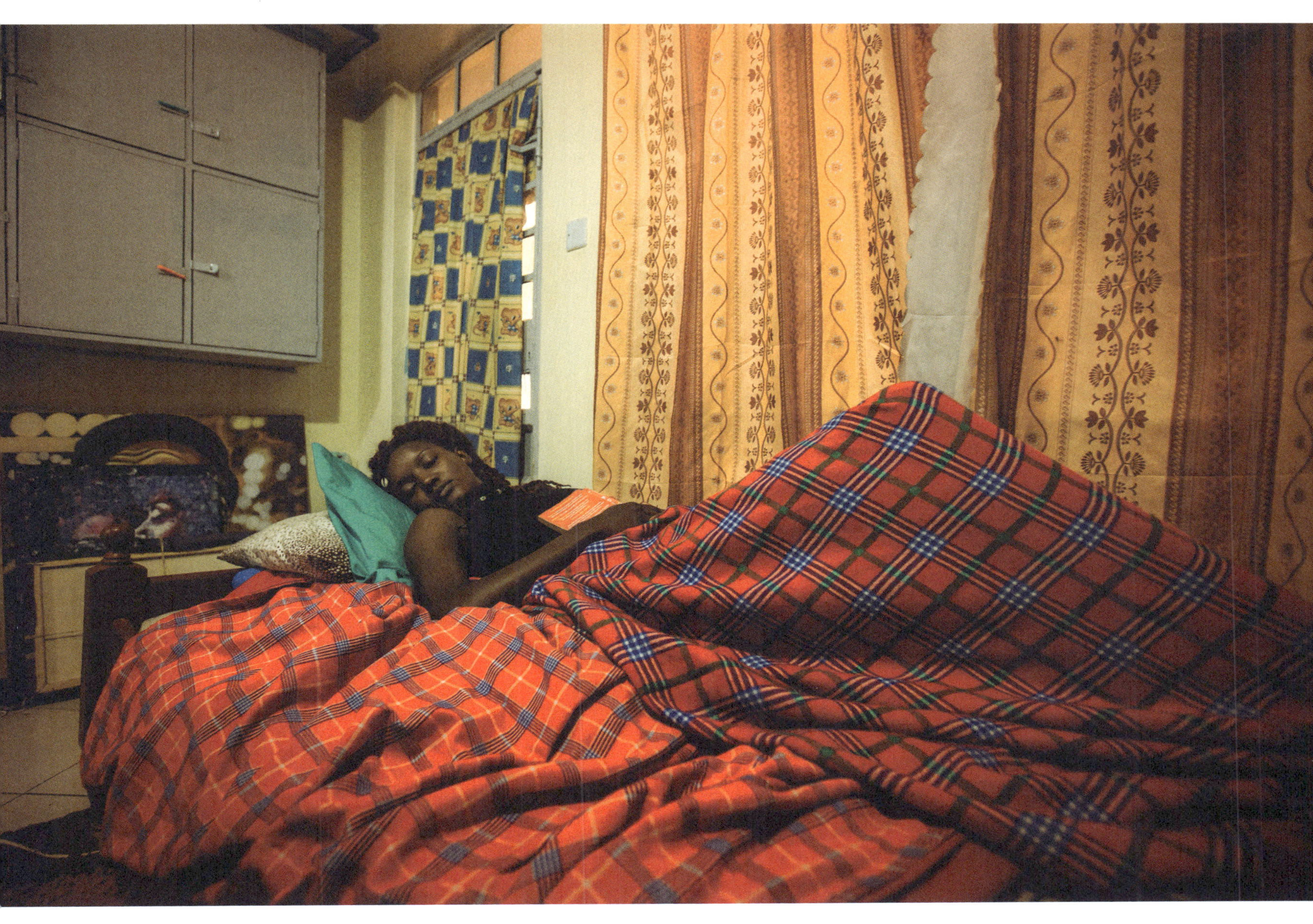

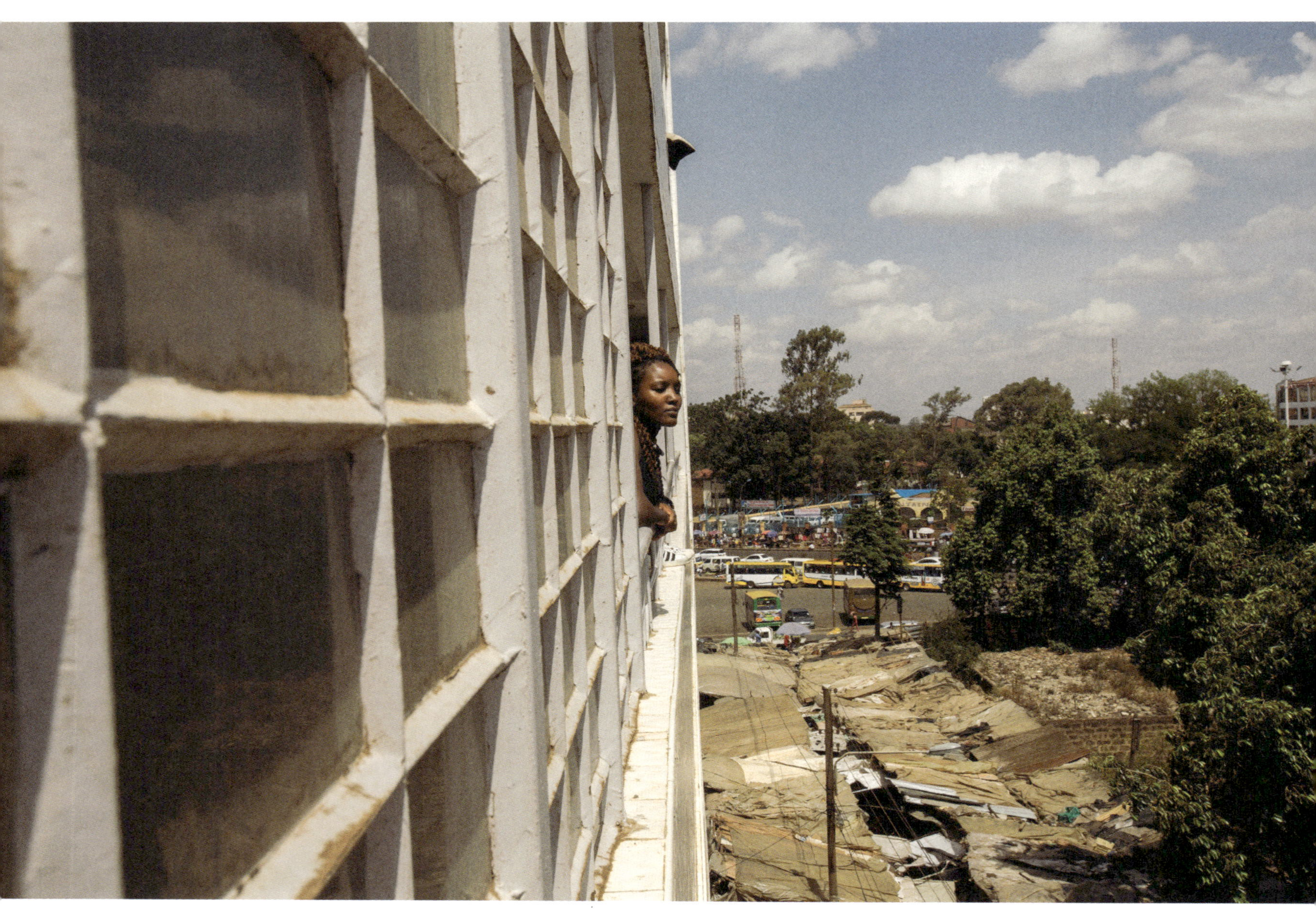

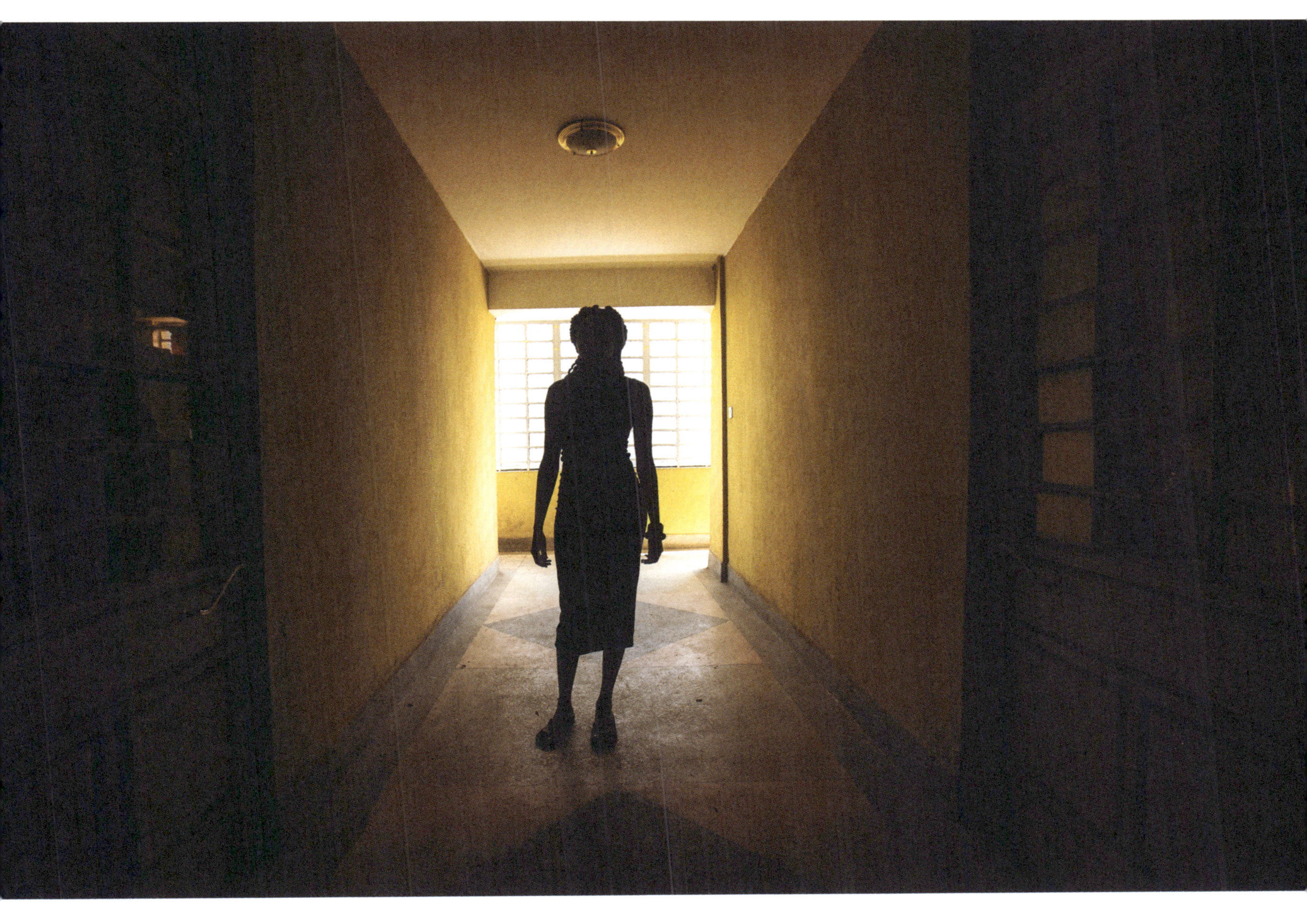

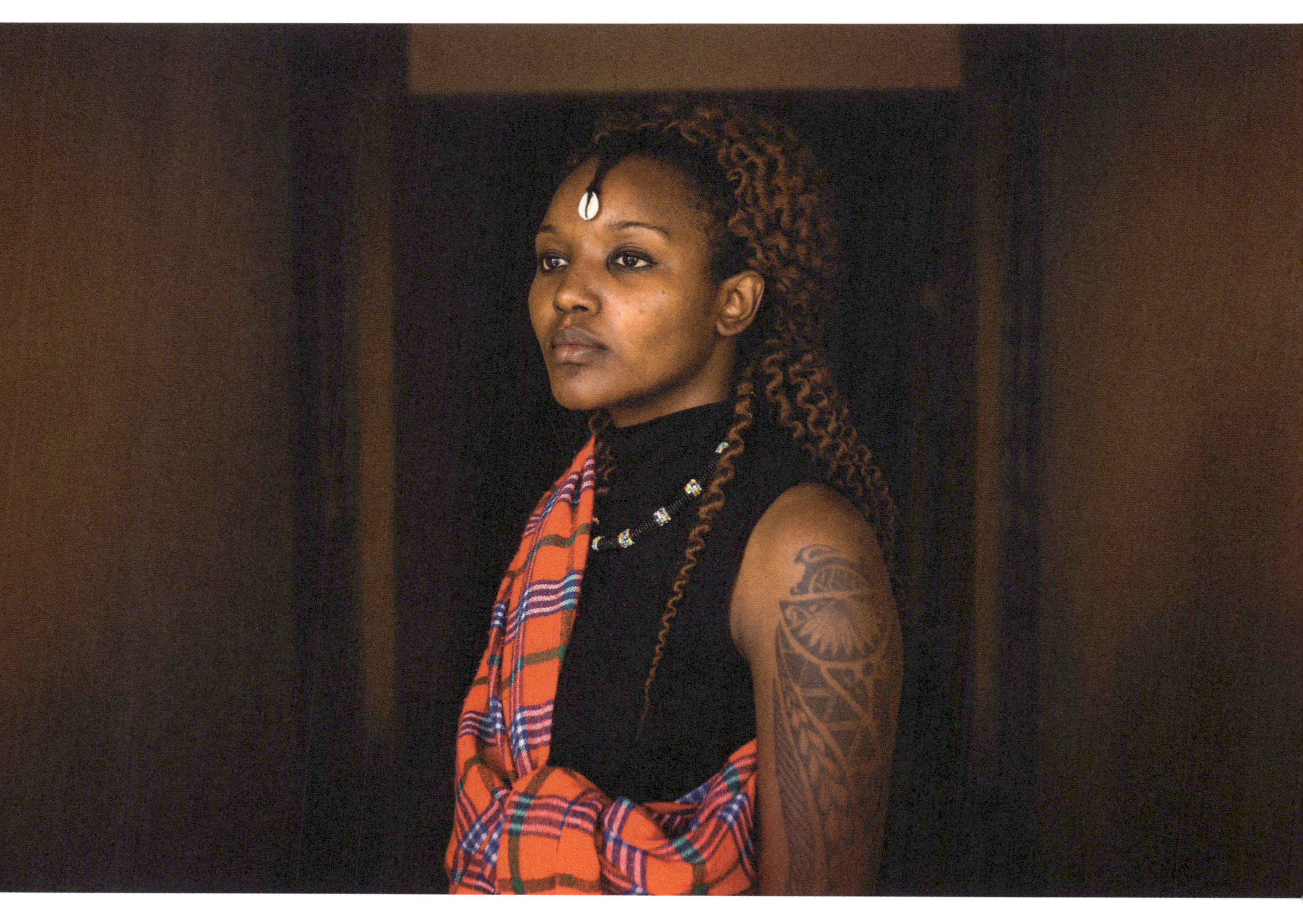

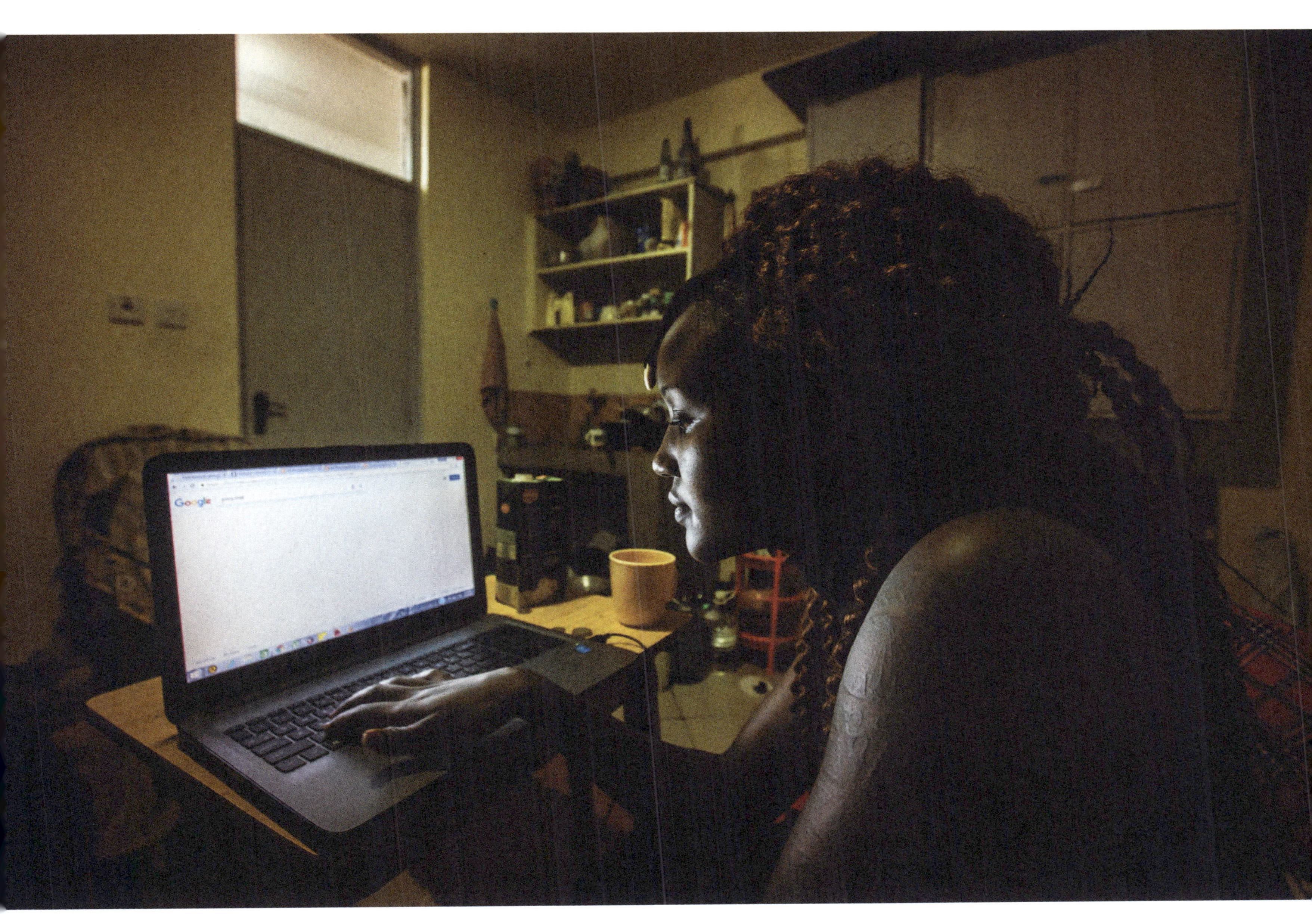
Google

Godlisten Meshack

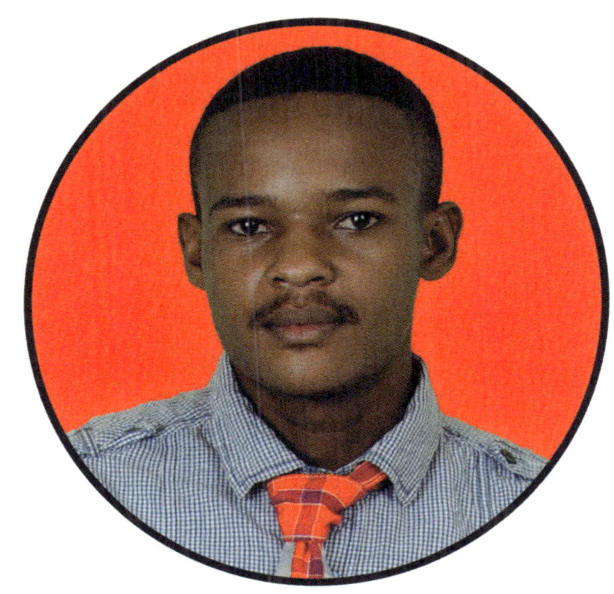

Grew up in: Arusha, Tanzania
Age: 26

(in collaboration with Perrine Philomeen)

26-year-old Godlisten Meshack who is himself Maasai from Arusha; a Northerly city in Tanzania that is replete with Maasai traders, businessmen and professionals is a trained video editor who actively distances himself from the stereotypical postcard image the Western world is obsessed with. For him, no matter how tightly bound he is to his cultural identity, presenting himself as a traditional Maasai is not only to fortify the single story malaise of Western media but it also limits his prospects of career development in today's competitive job scene. He enlisted the help of a Dutch fashion design student to craft inventive ways of bringing together elements from western style clothing and traditional Maasai garments as a way of neutralising the conflict that raged inside him.

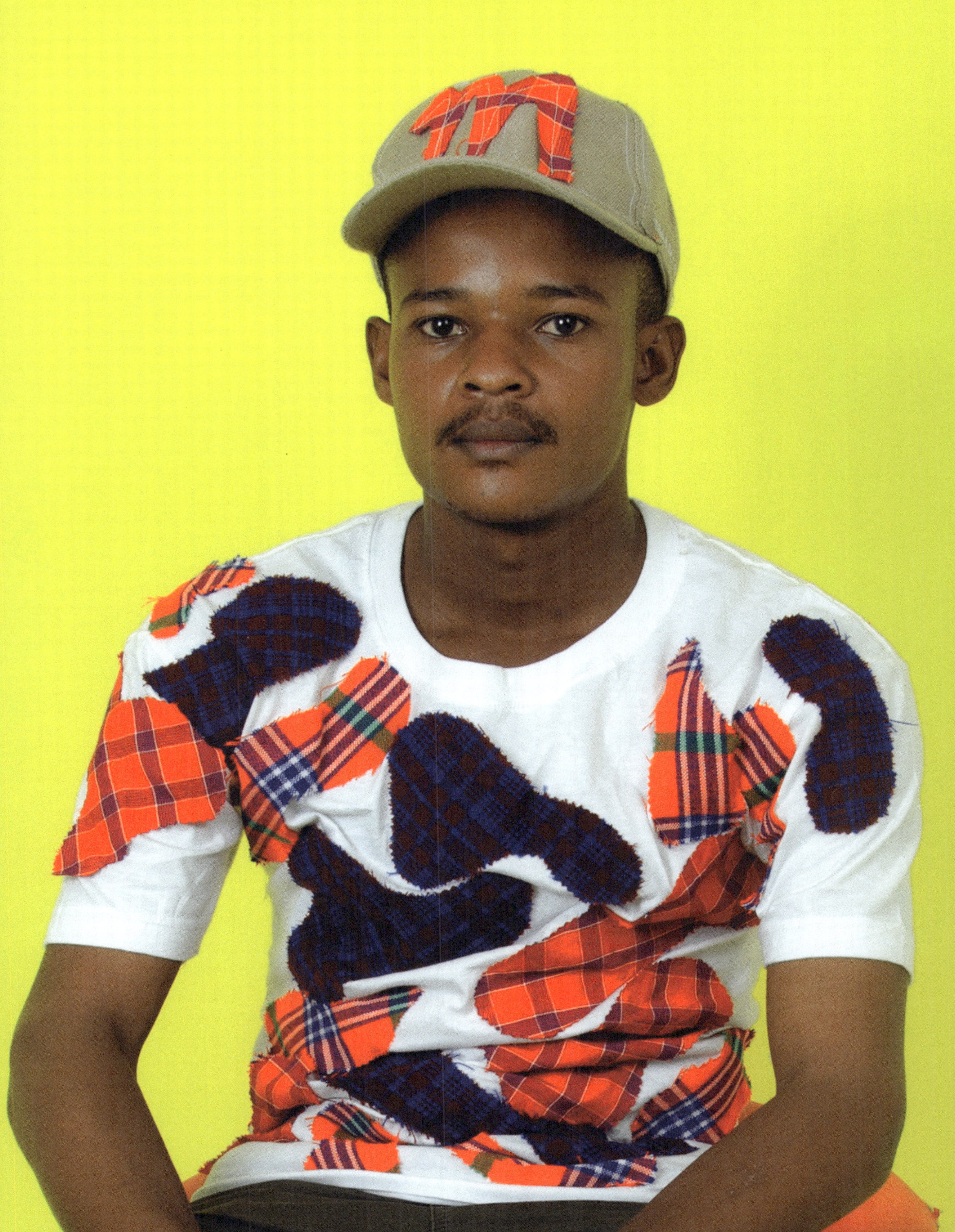

John Obiero

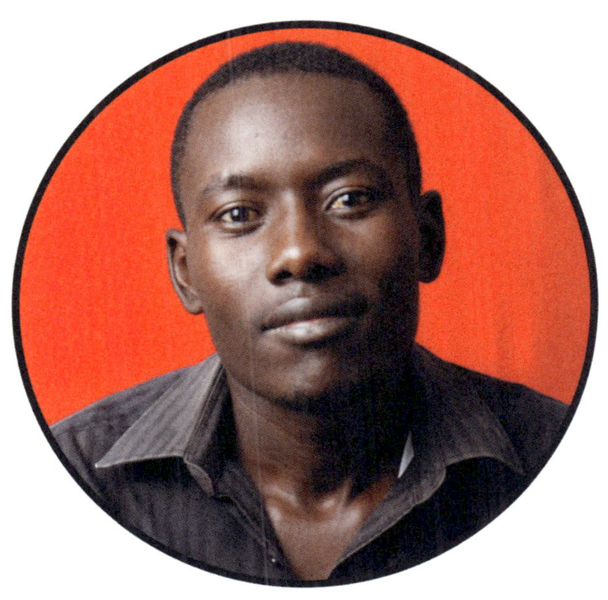

Grew up in: Homa Bay

Age: 24

Convinced that many external factors have made the evolution of architecture among the traditional Maasai inevitable, John Obiero documents shifts in the way Maa people are living today. Whether influenced by a change in economic status or the disappearance of once locally available materials, John recognises that things have definitely changed since he visited a Maasai village during a school trip and saw for himself the inside of a traditional Manyatta; an adventure he does not particularly care to experience ever again.

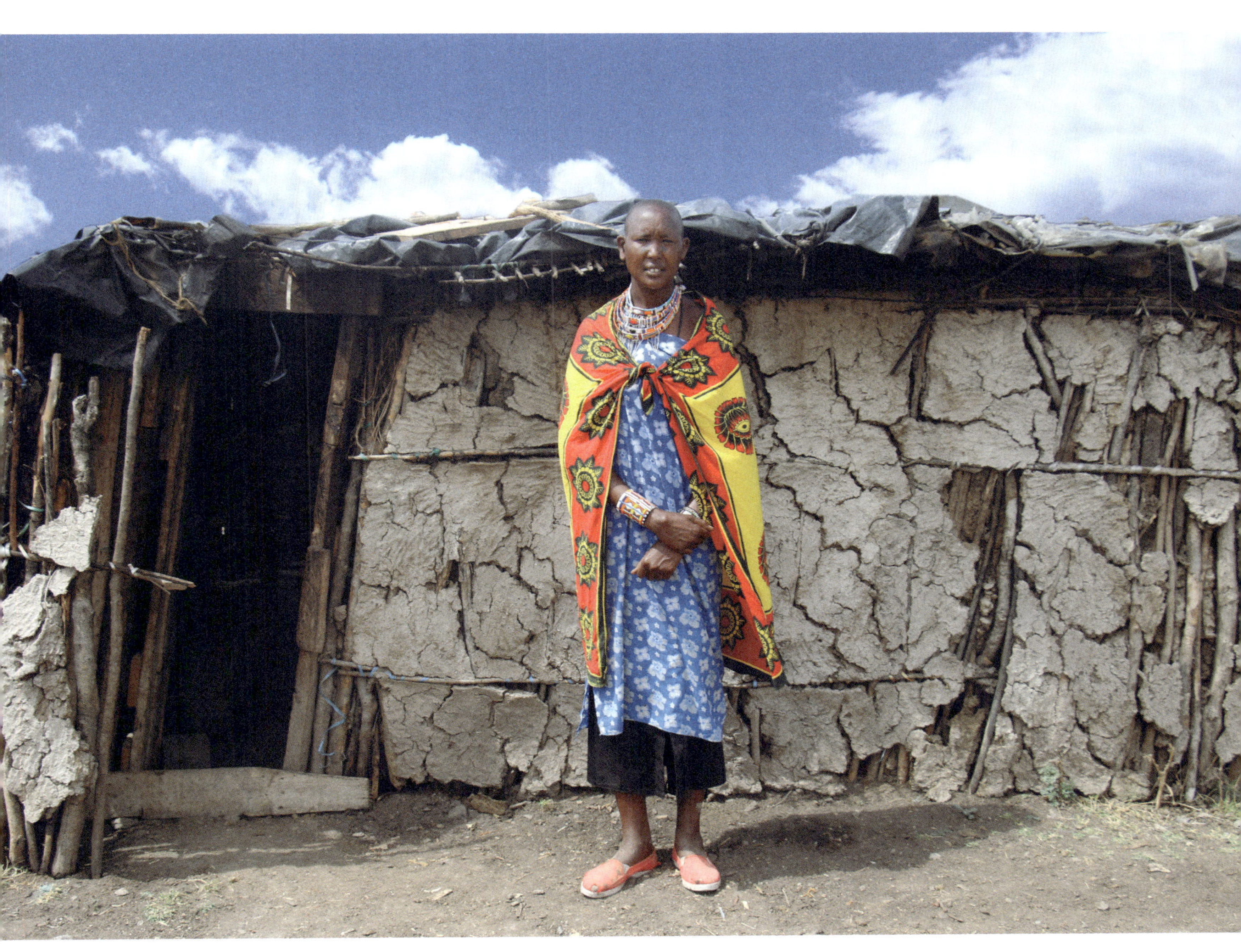

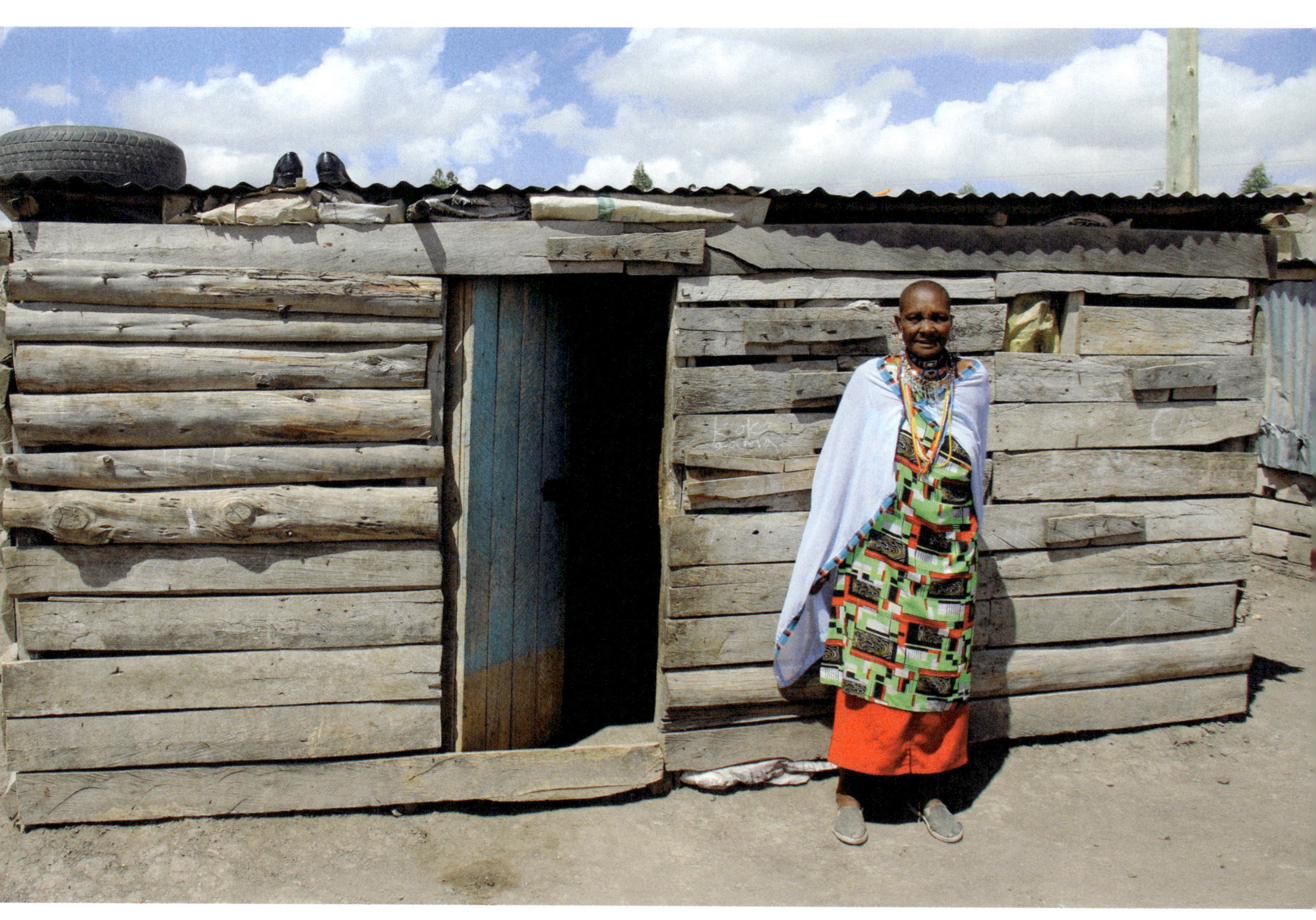

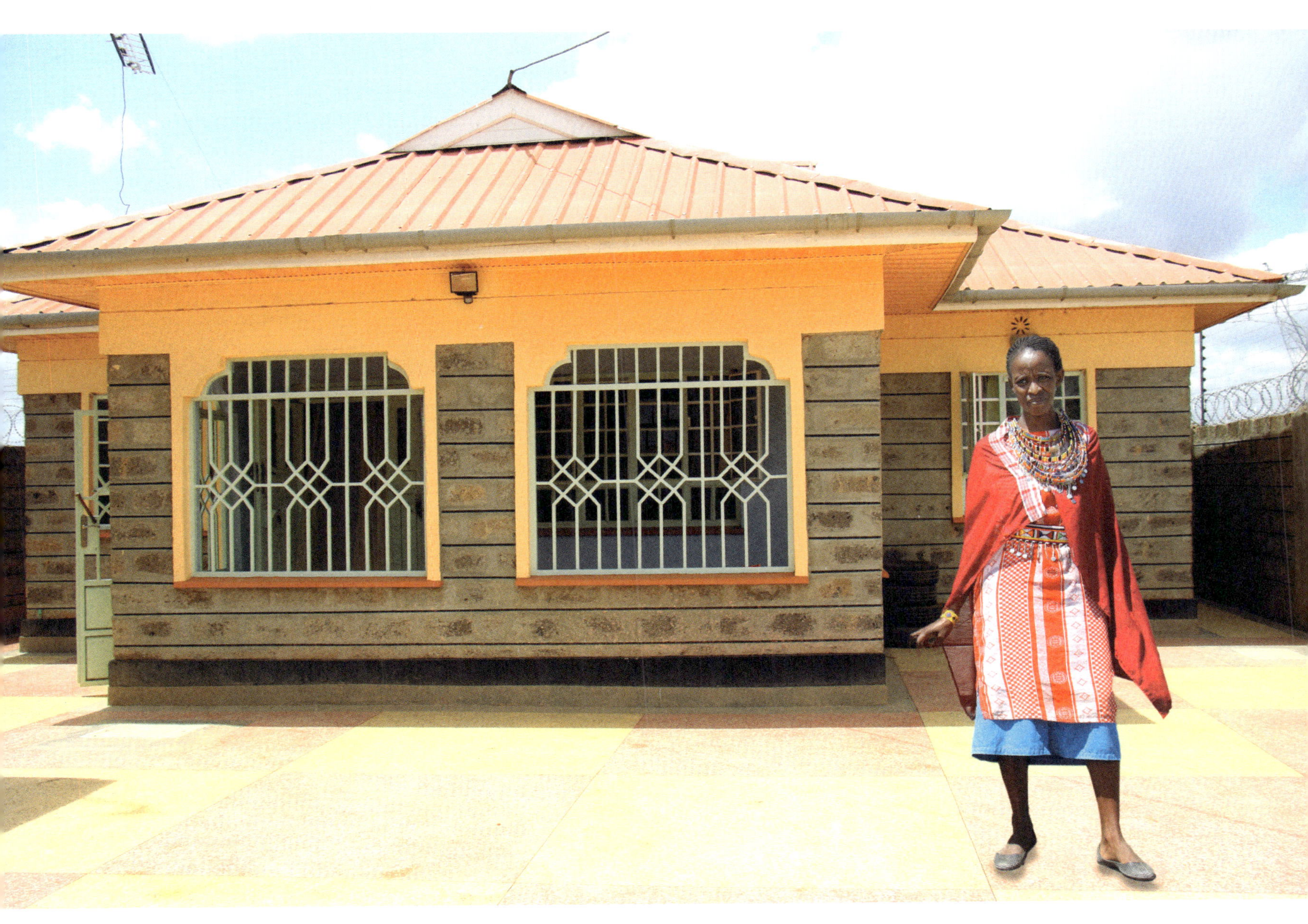

Malcolm Nduati

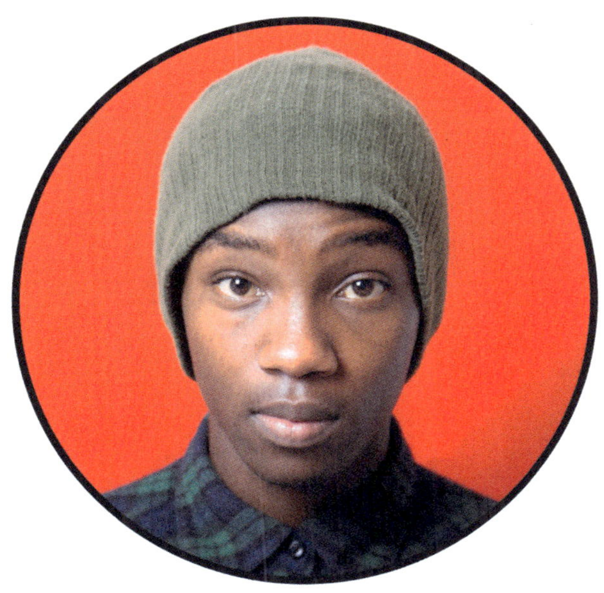

Grew up in: Nakuru

Age: 18

In his days as a high school student, Malcolm Nduati was an insufferable bully whose actions were especially cruel towards his Maasai counterparts. So invested in dehumanising the Maa boys at school was his gang that they adopted a derogatory name for them: 'Ndaghuo' (slang denoting foolishness or cluelessness). A year ago he watched the performance of a guest artiste at his local church that blew him away. The young rapper was talented and hip with even more 'swagger' than Malcolm who is himself an underground rapper/photographer. But what was more shocking is that he was Maasai! This discovery of Maa people in mainstream entertainment shook up Malcolm's entire outlook and he has found other rappers from the Maasai community to collaborate with both musically and in his photography.

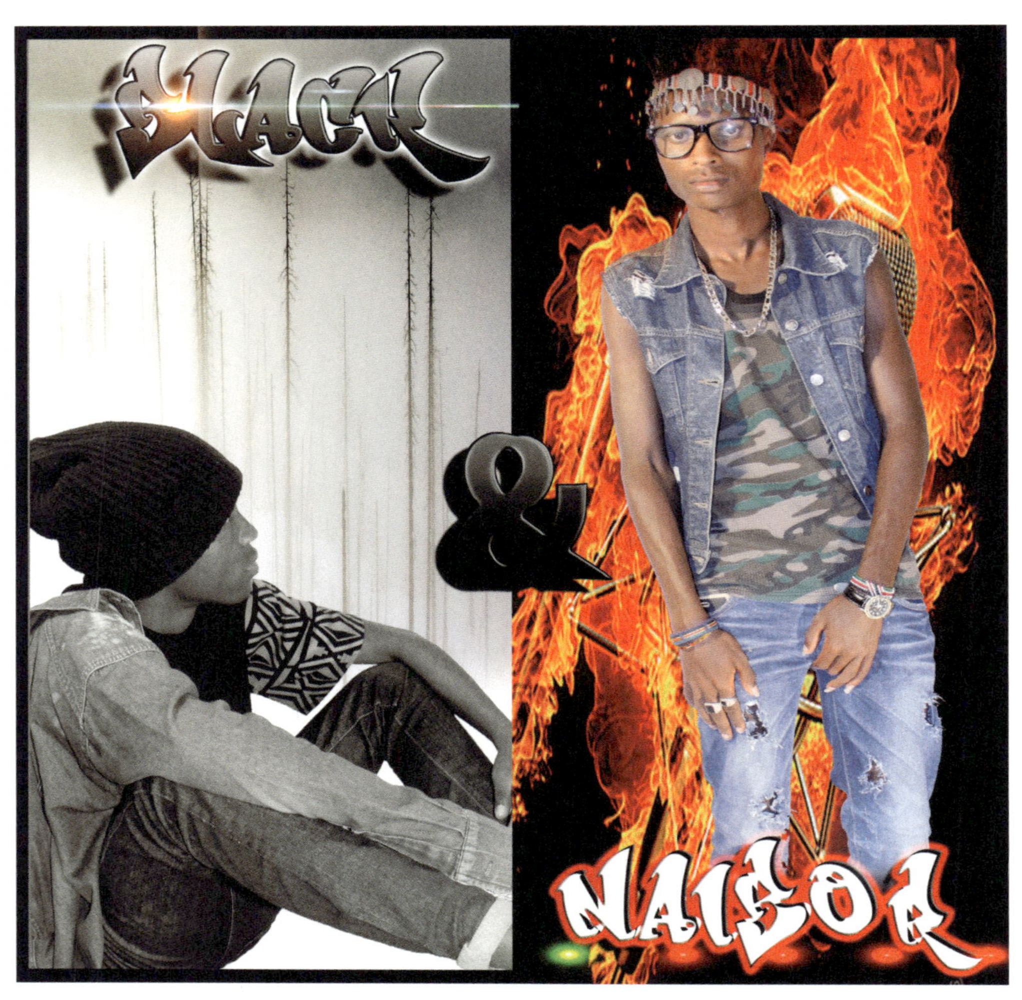
BLACK
&
NAIBOR

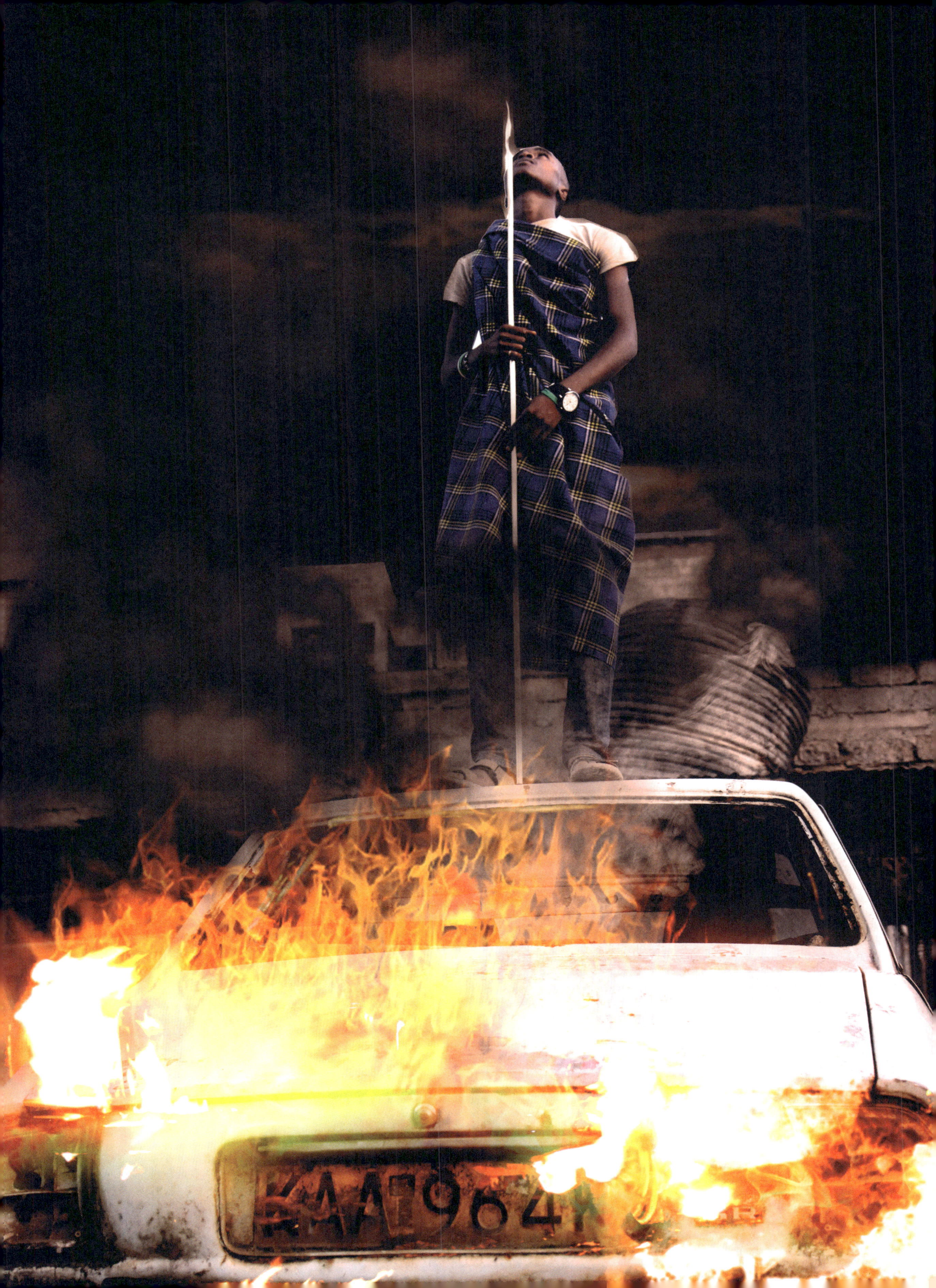

Celine Mwangi

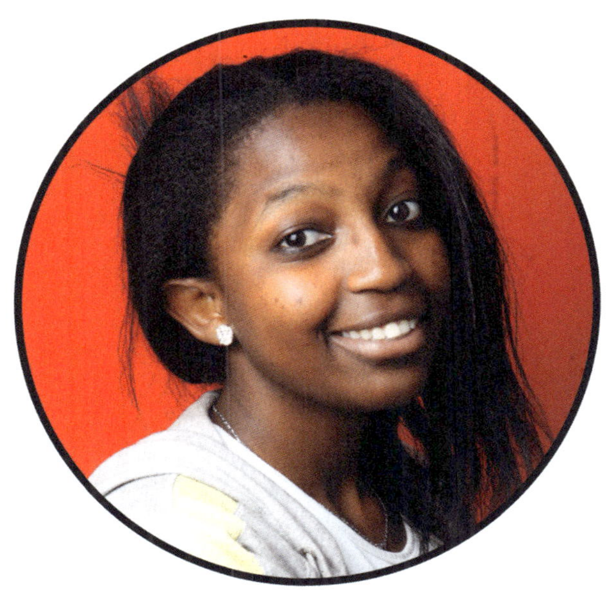

Grew up in: Nairobi
Age: 18

While it is indeed true that traditionally, the Maa were a feared warrior tribe, today they are no more a threat than any other ethnic group trying to preserve itself in treacherous times. Celine Mwangi has only ever been exposed to the reductionist narrative of how murderous the Maa people are. With this work, she chooses to help rewrite the story of the Maa by showing us an unexpected tenderness from her subjects who many would be surprised to know have never been in the battlefield.

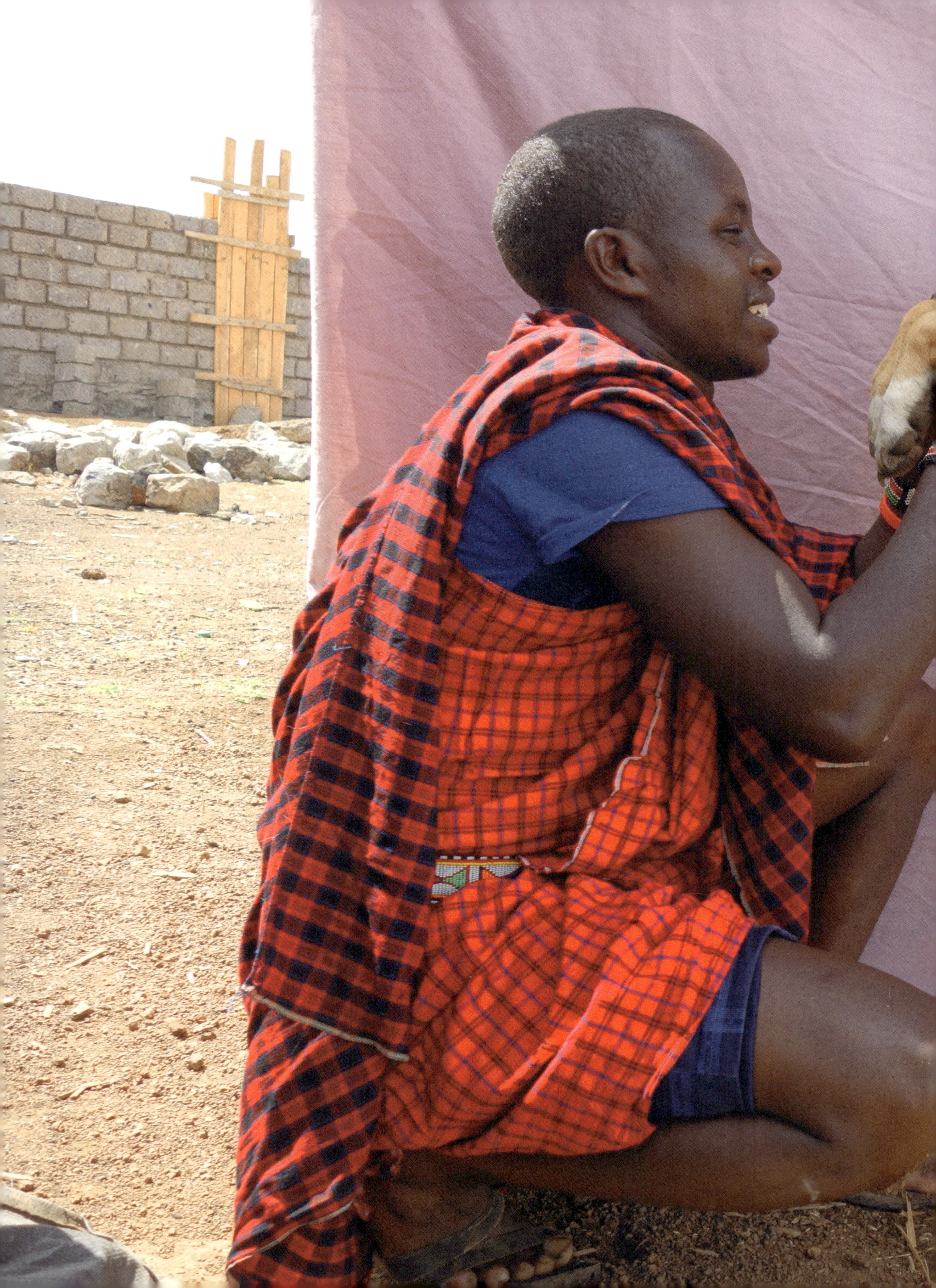

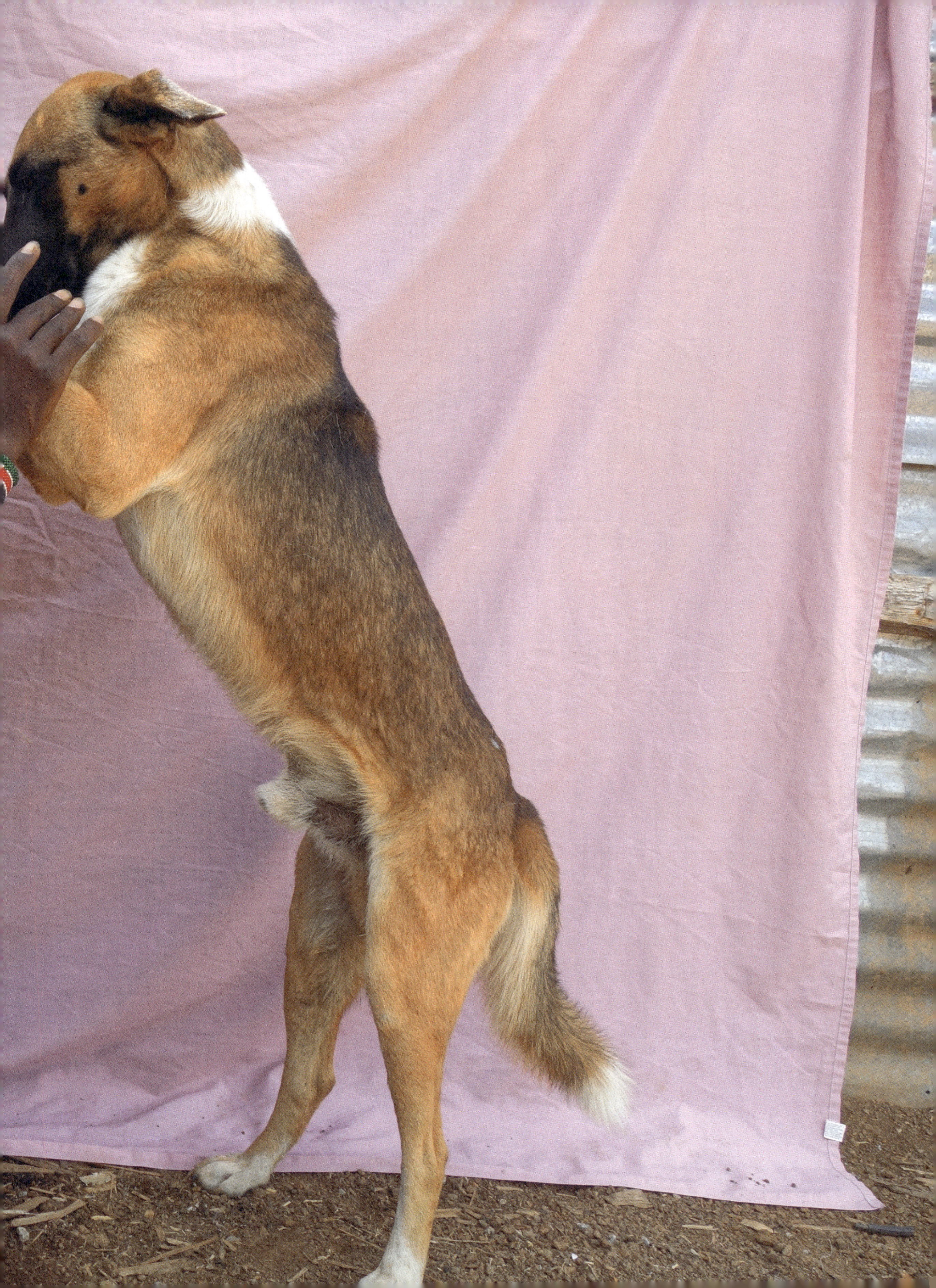

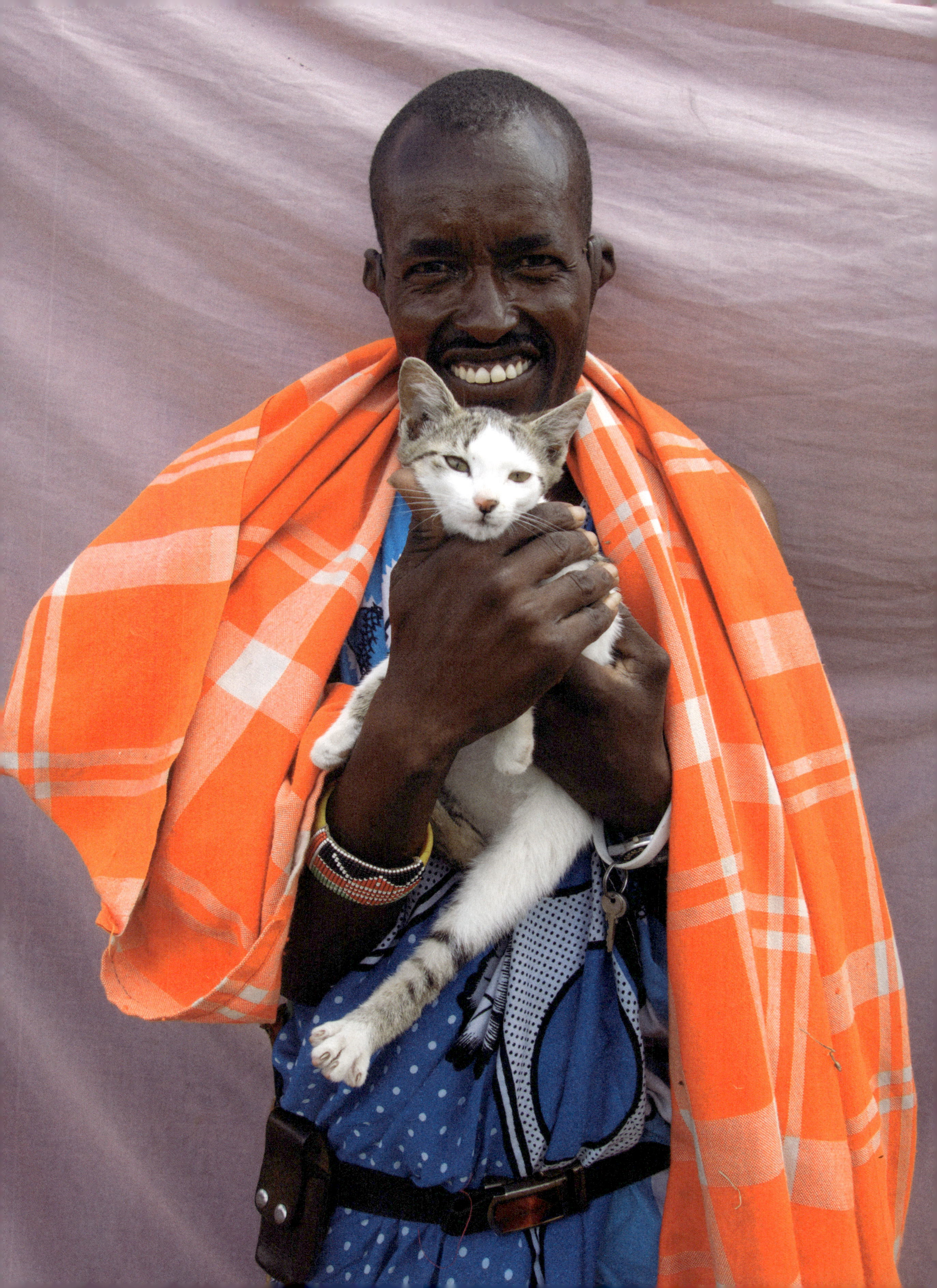

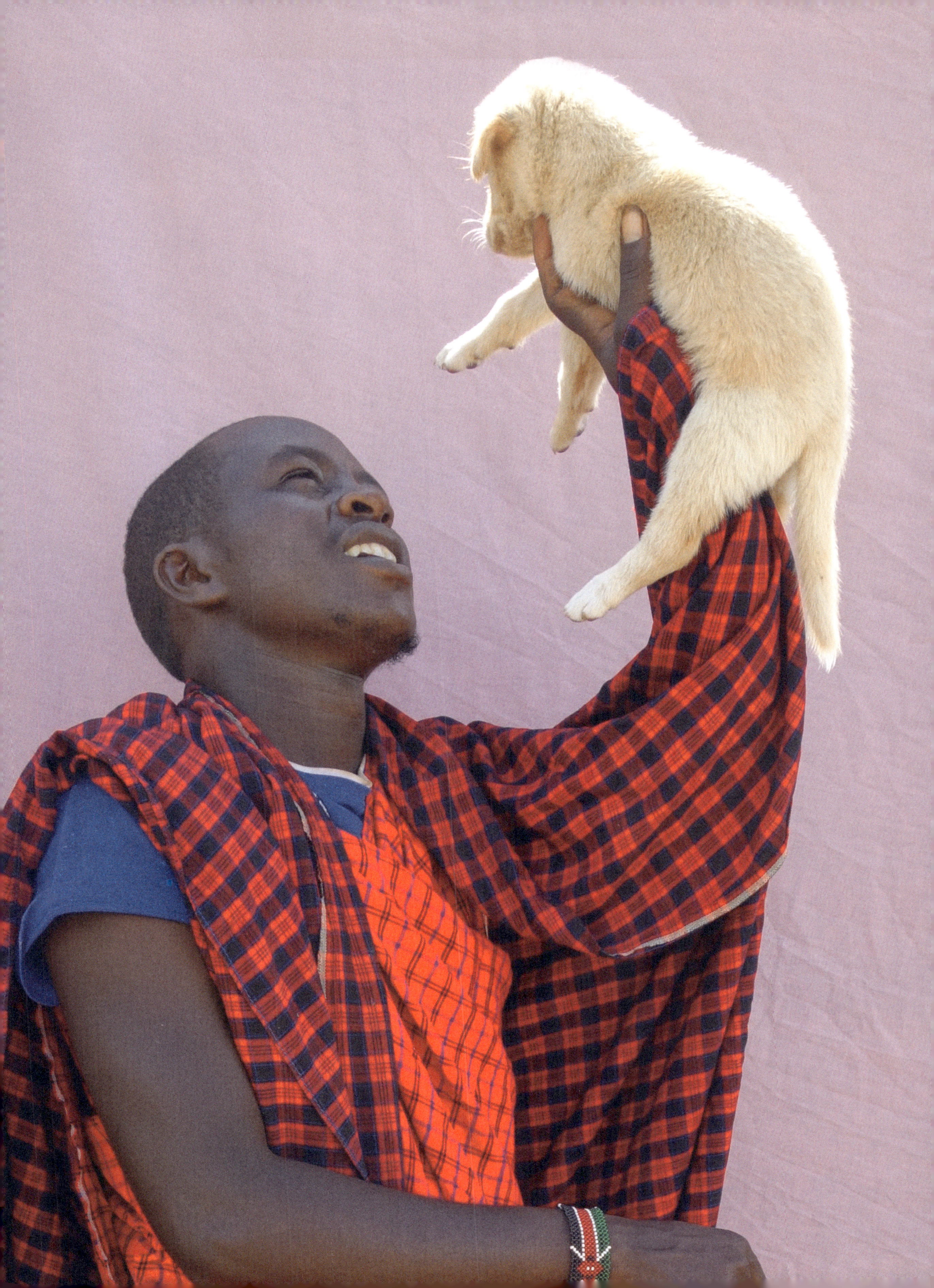

Jeffa Kombe

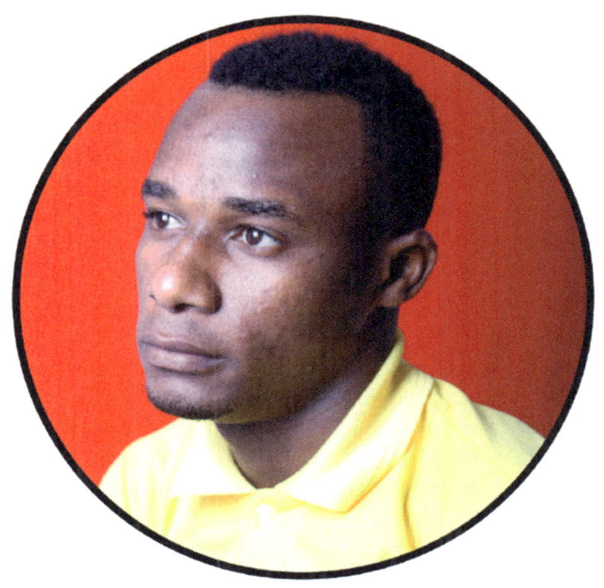

Grew up in: Nyango, Kwale County
Age: 20

Death rituals and the motions experienced by those affected by death are universal occurrences which while bespoken in nuanced ways remain equally significant across races and creeds. Jeffa Kombe grew up in a remote village in the coastal region of Kenya with a large Maasai community whose cultural practices surrounding bereavement he observed closely. He appreciates that some of the more macabre rites of the past have been replaced with more modern ones but still, strands of the olden practices remain. Because this photographic journey shuttled Jeffa to many emotional places as he looked into the grieving processes in Maa communities, there is an almost poetic structure to the composition of his images which reflects his state at the time.

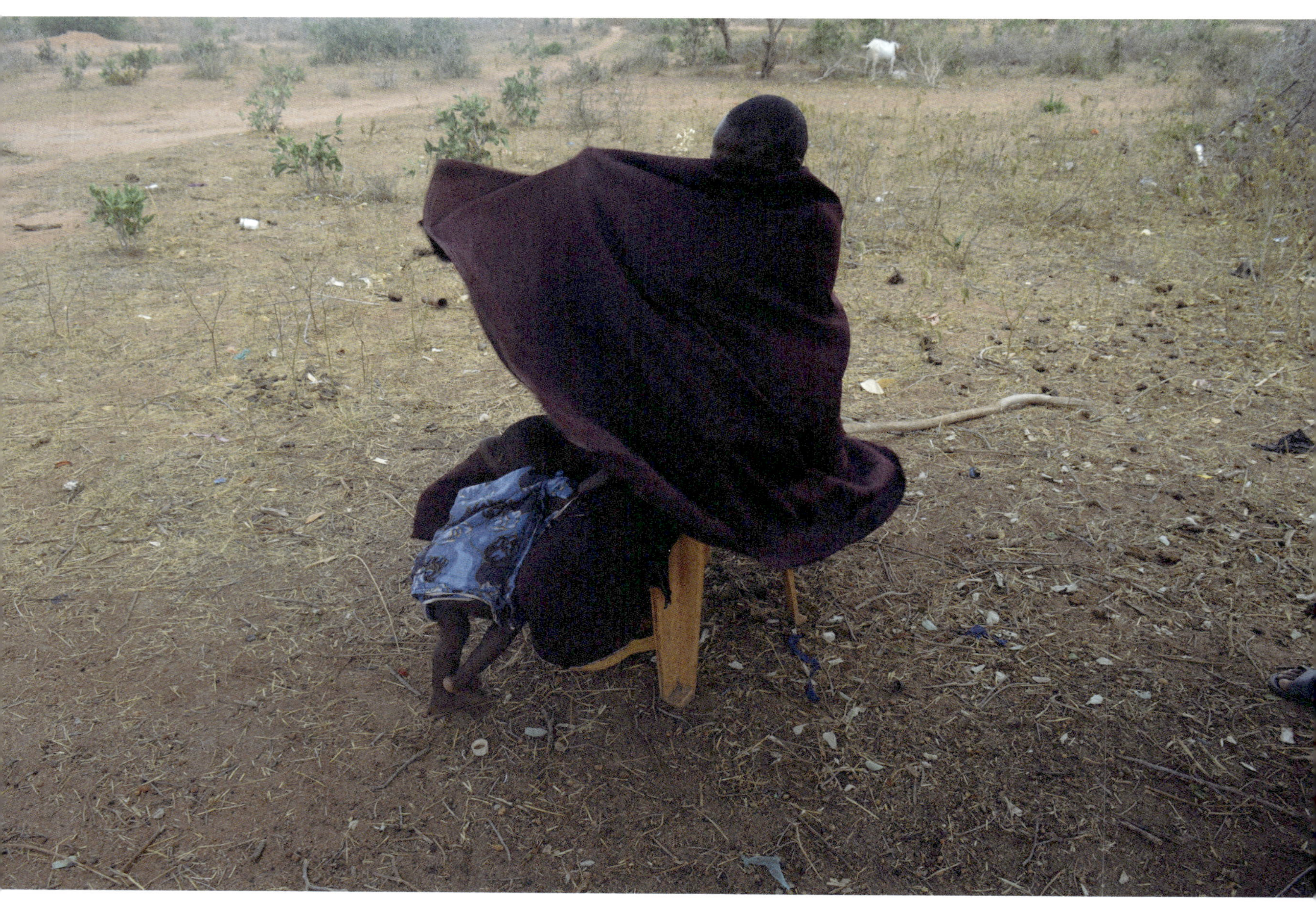

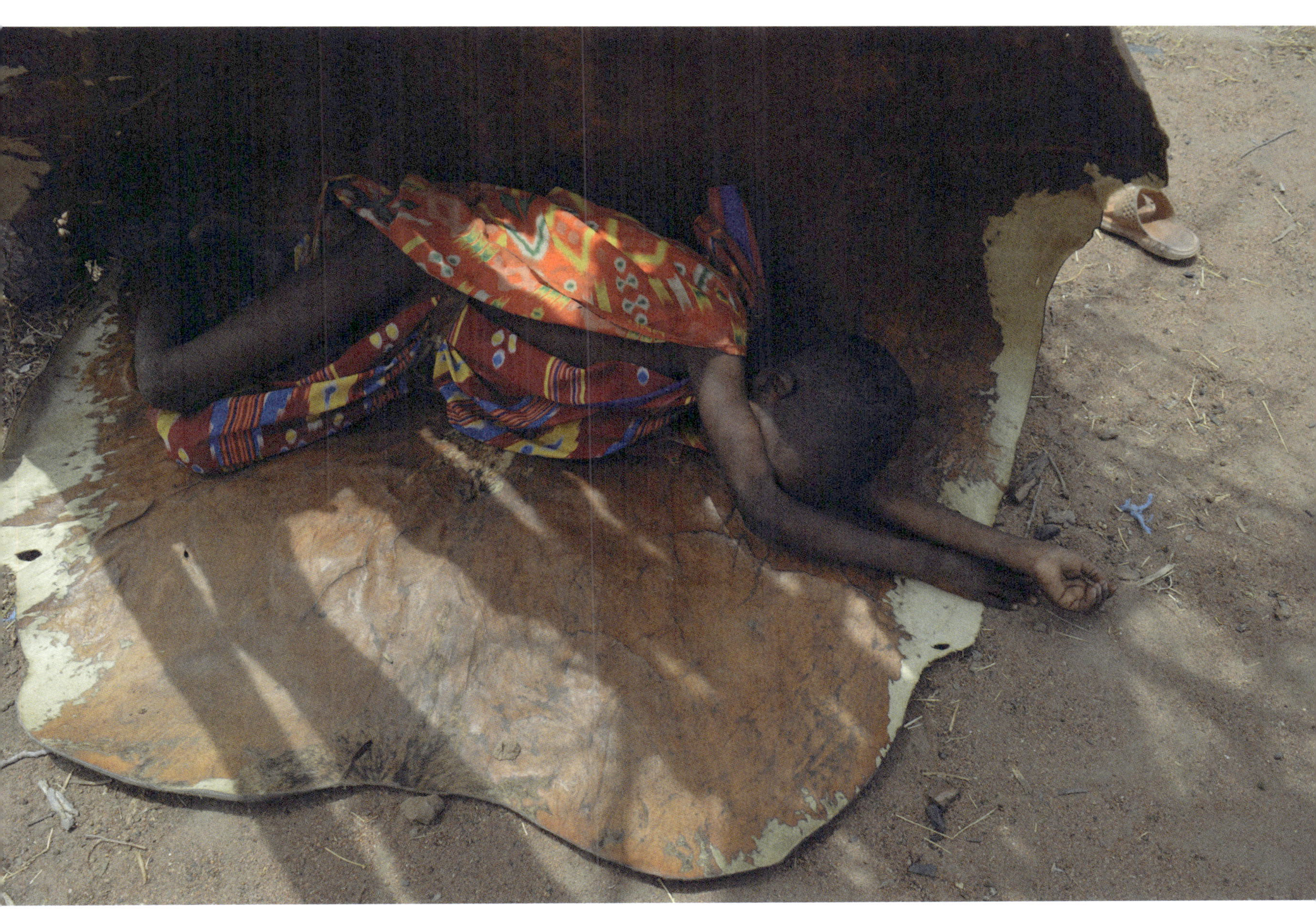

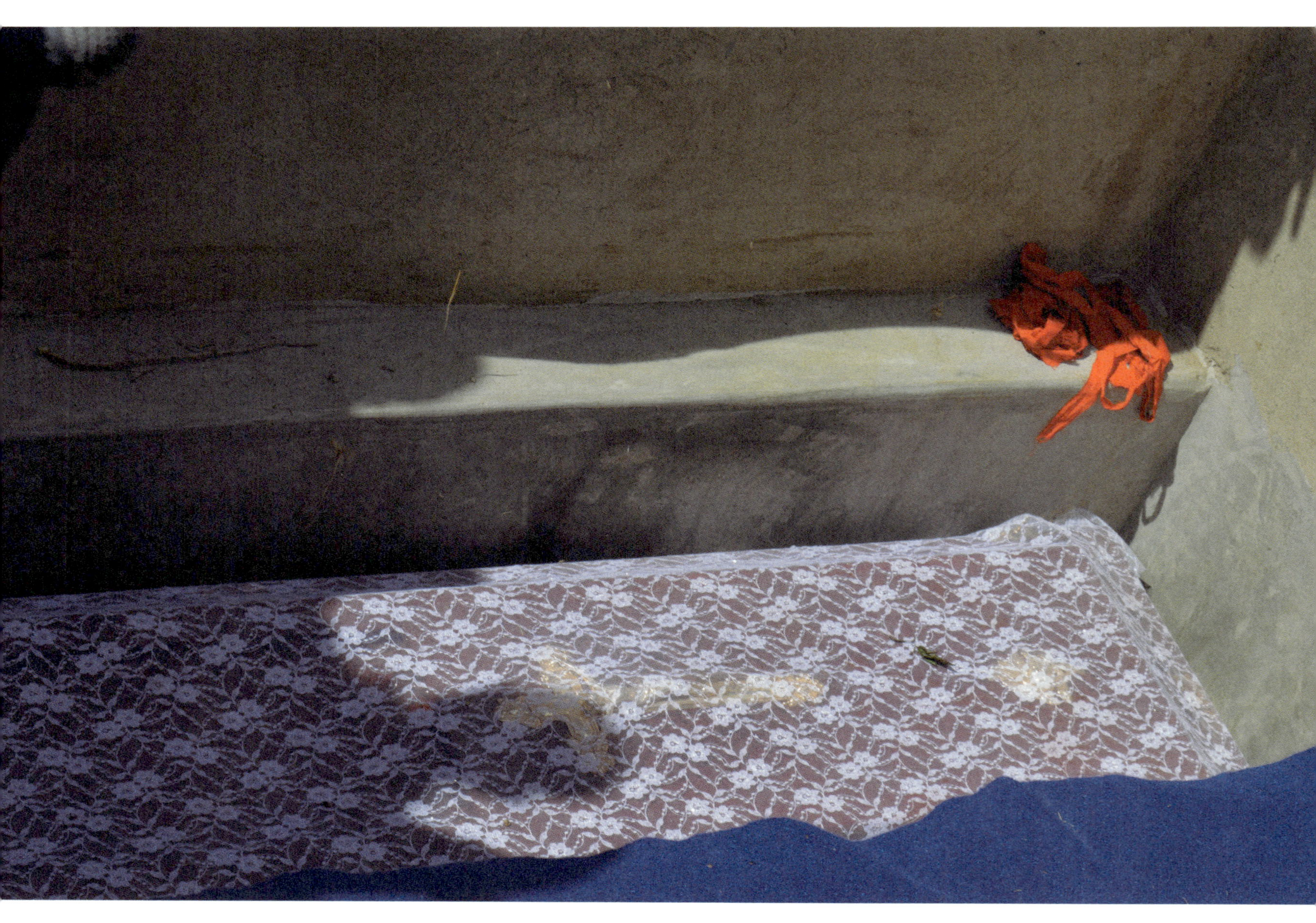

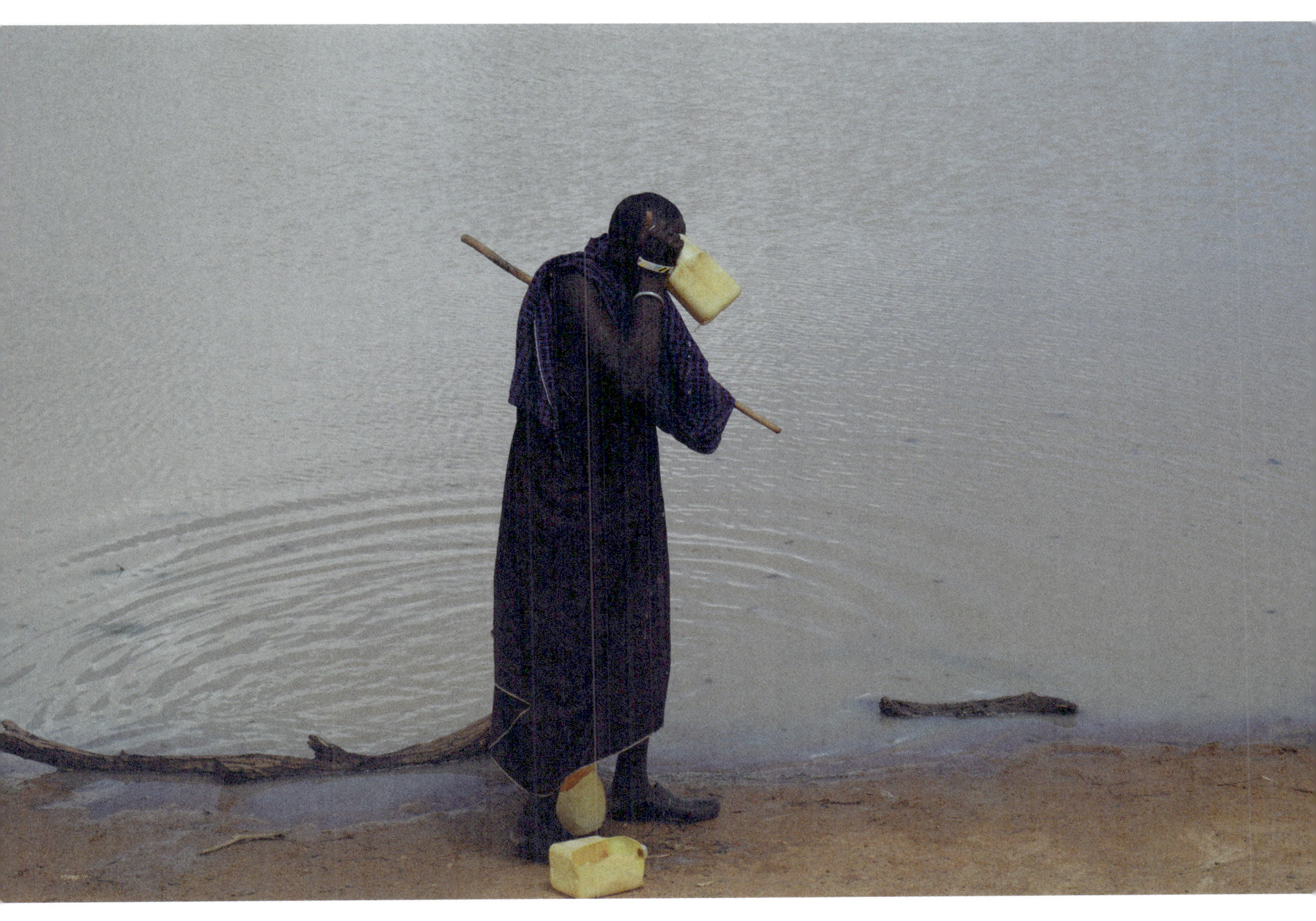

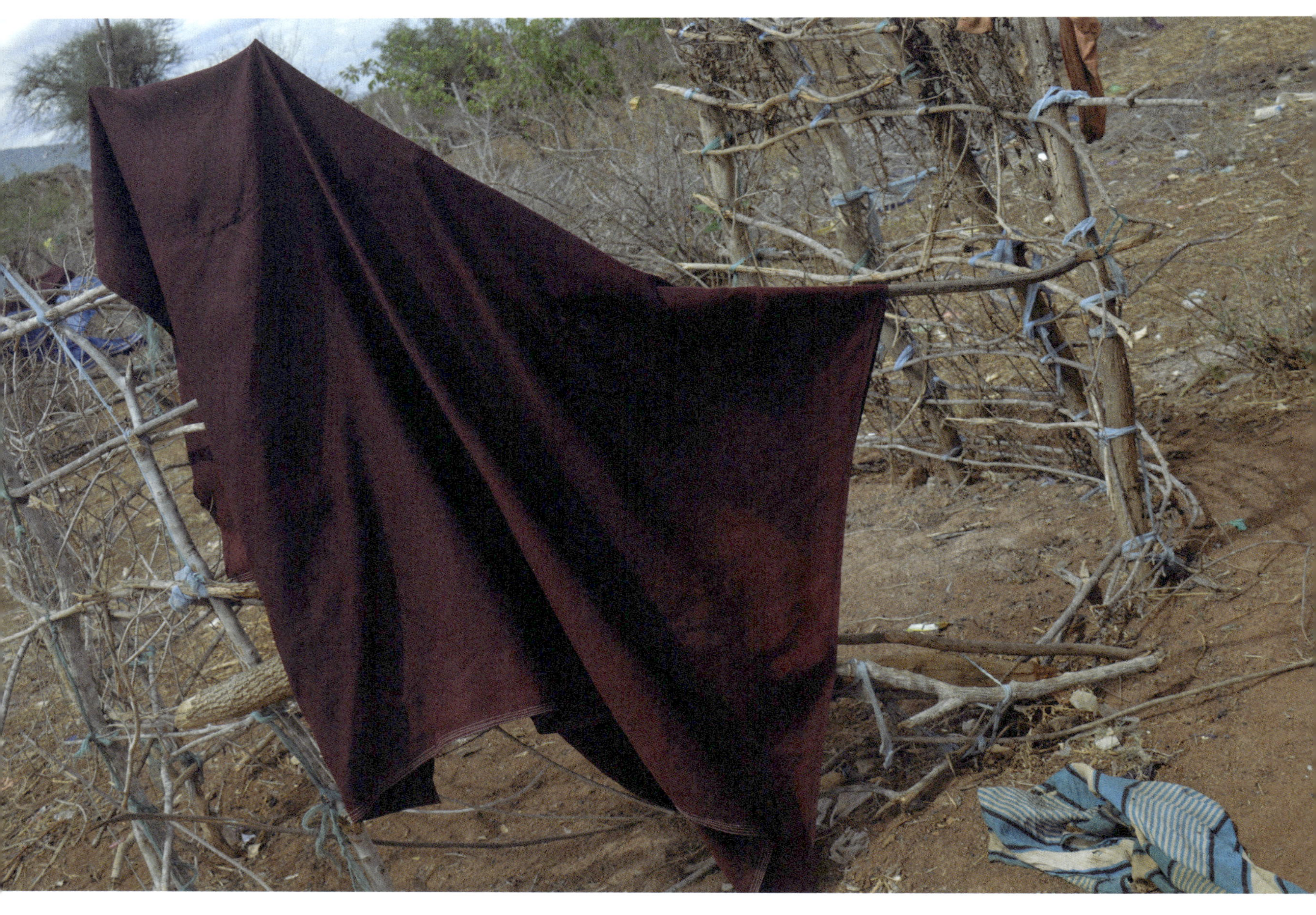

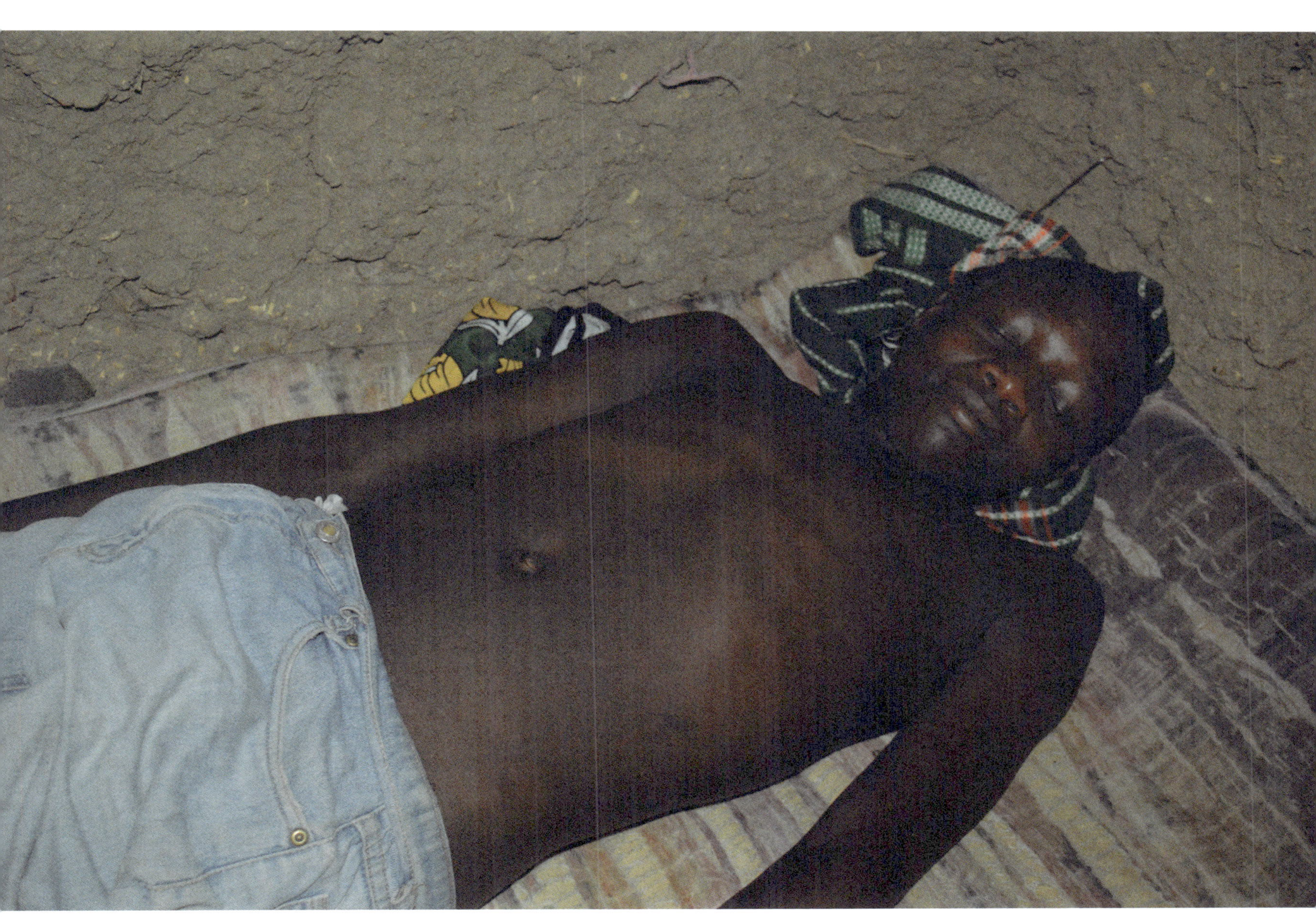

Sarah Waiswa

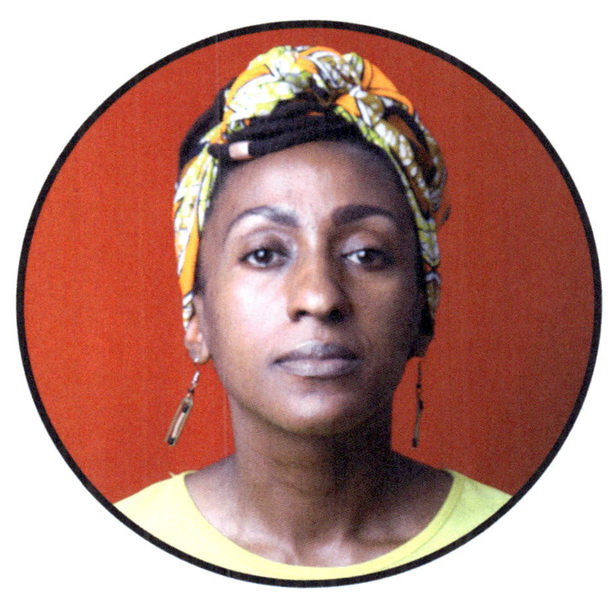

Grew up in: Nairobi
Age: 36

For Sarah Waiswa, a Uganda born Kenya based industry heavyweight, creative expression is a most organic phenomenon so when she started on this project, it was with more unknowing than knowing. One time, listening to the legend of a long forgotten female deity from a time before modern religion came to the shores of Africa, she was overcome with an intellectual curiosity.
How could a society so deeply patriarchal have a history that is so opposite to the present? Sarah then investigated the subject and found there was little recorded information about this Pasinaai who was said to deliver livestock from the heavens. The photographer returned to the very village where she first heard the story of the female god and through her creative genius and ability to conceptualise and visualise, she gave Pasinaai a new breath of life as a fierce and strong woman in a place where opportunities for women to reach their full potential are few and far between.

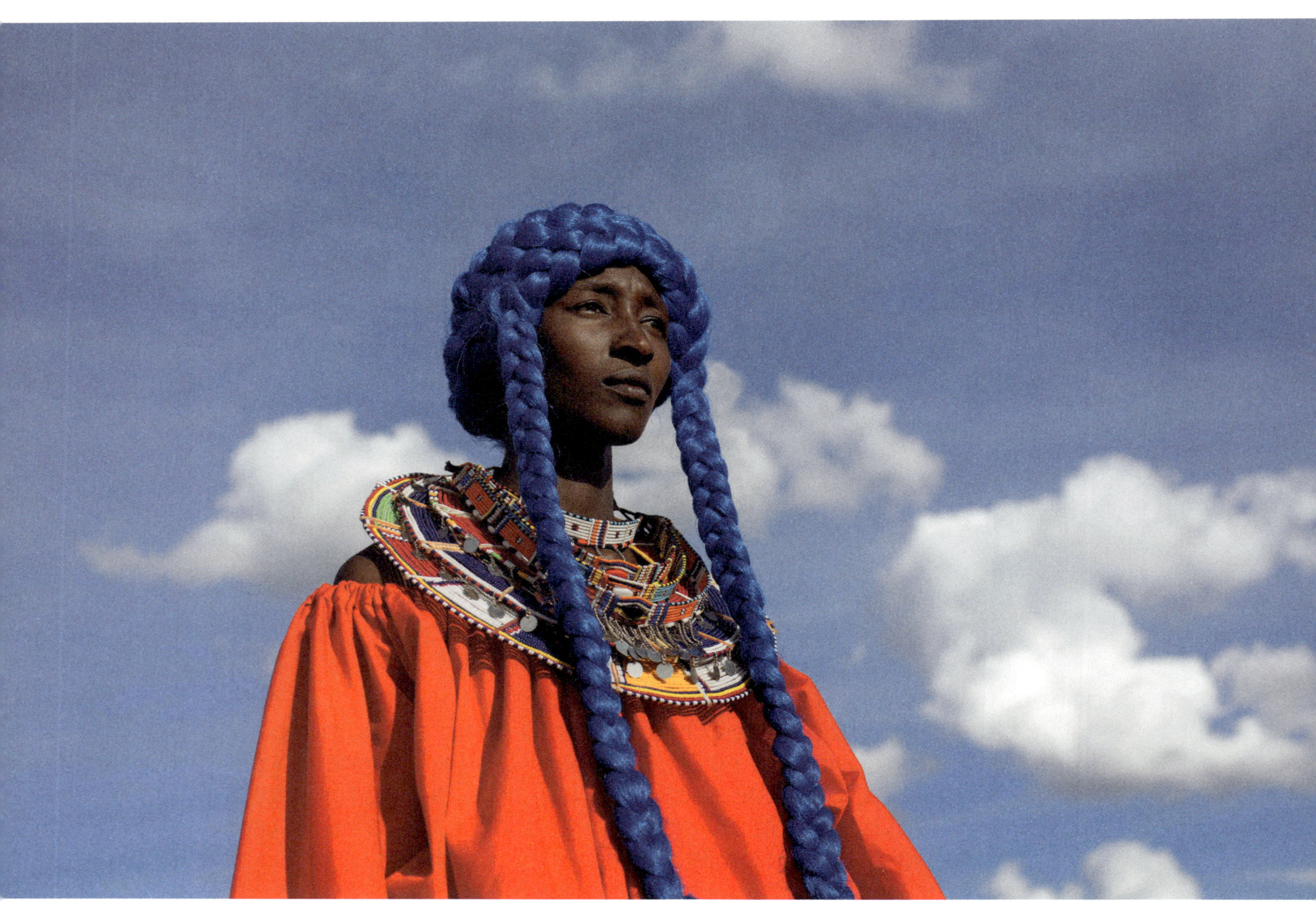

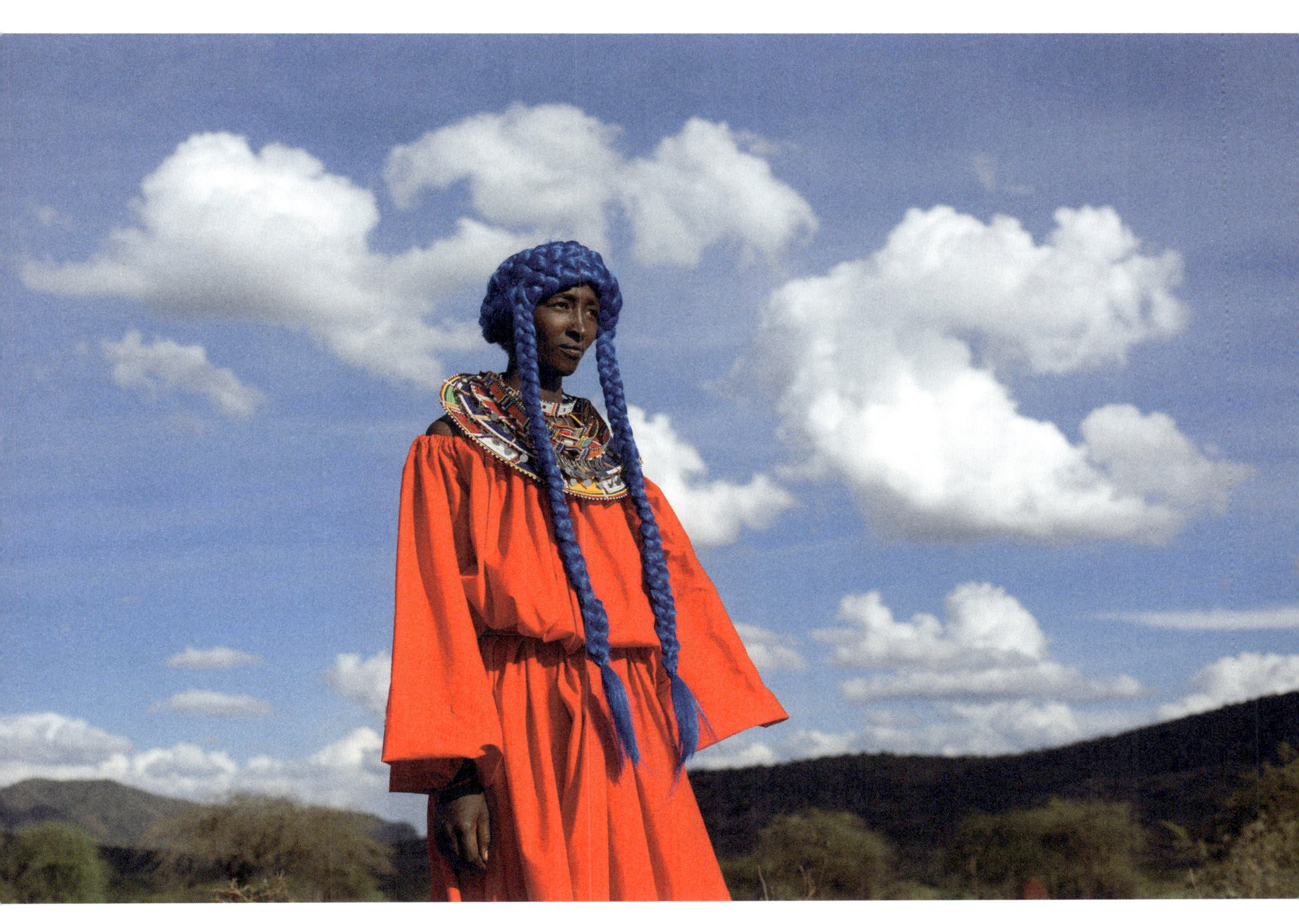

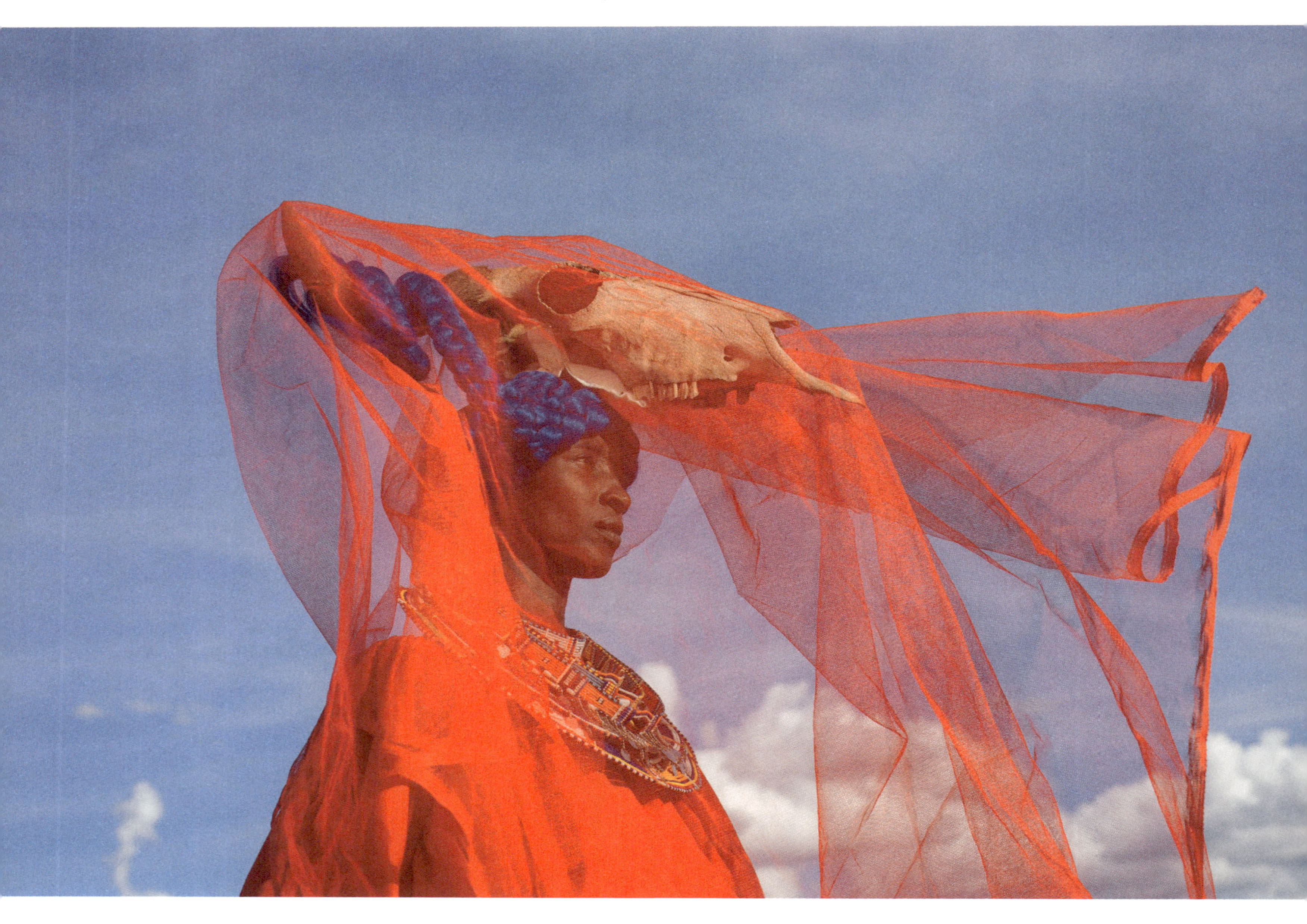

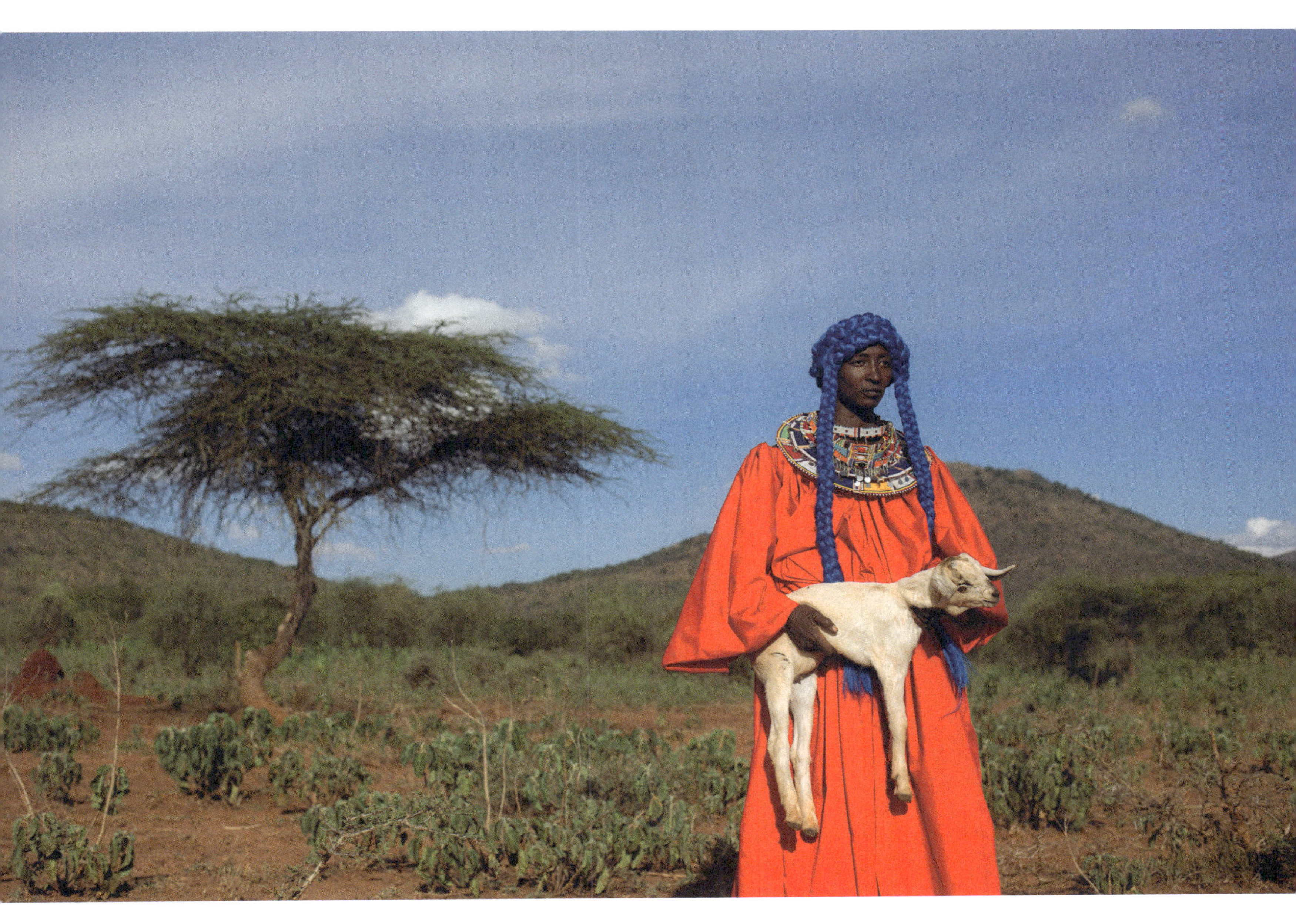

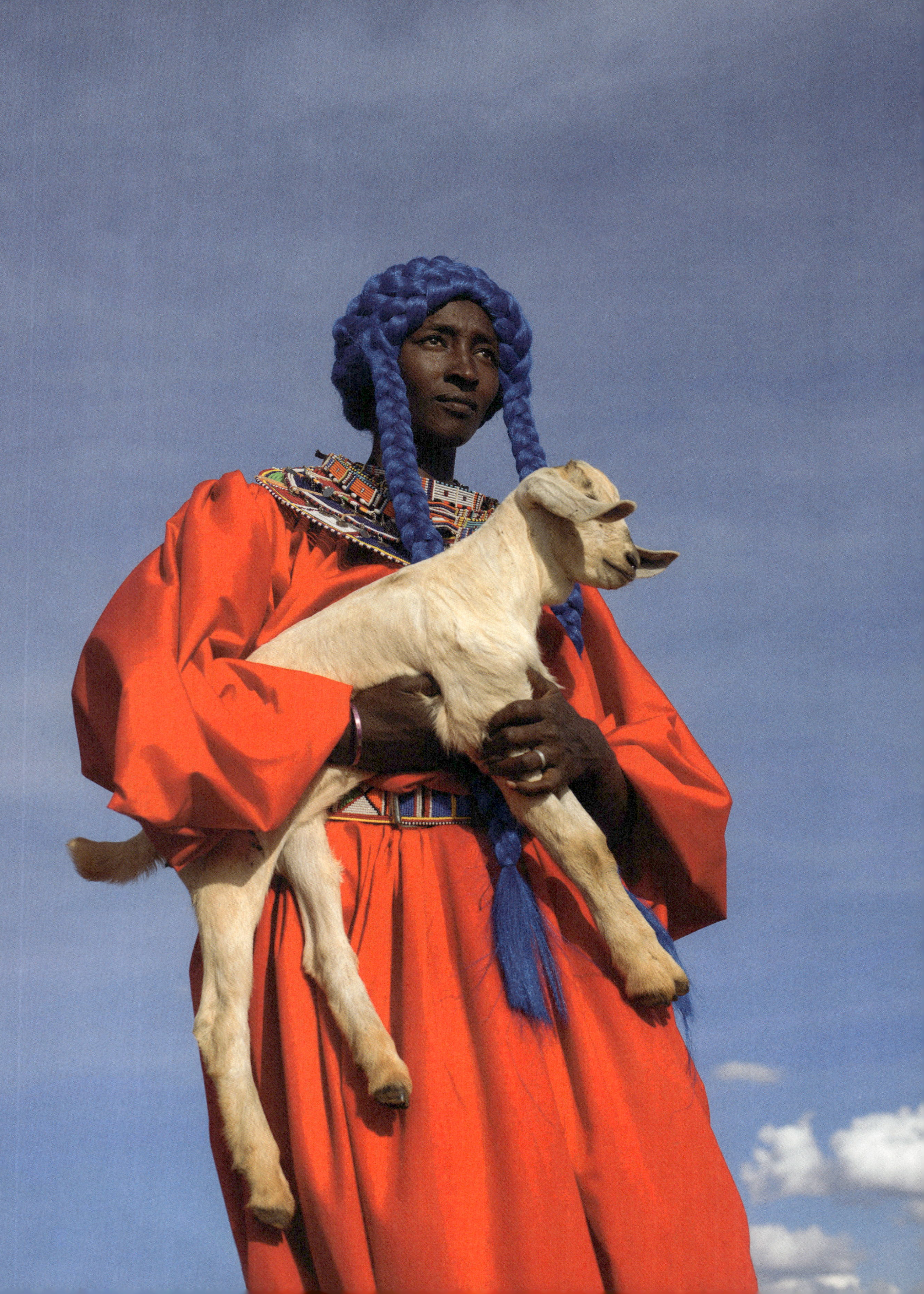

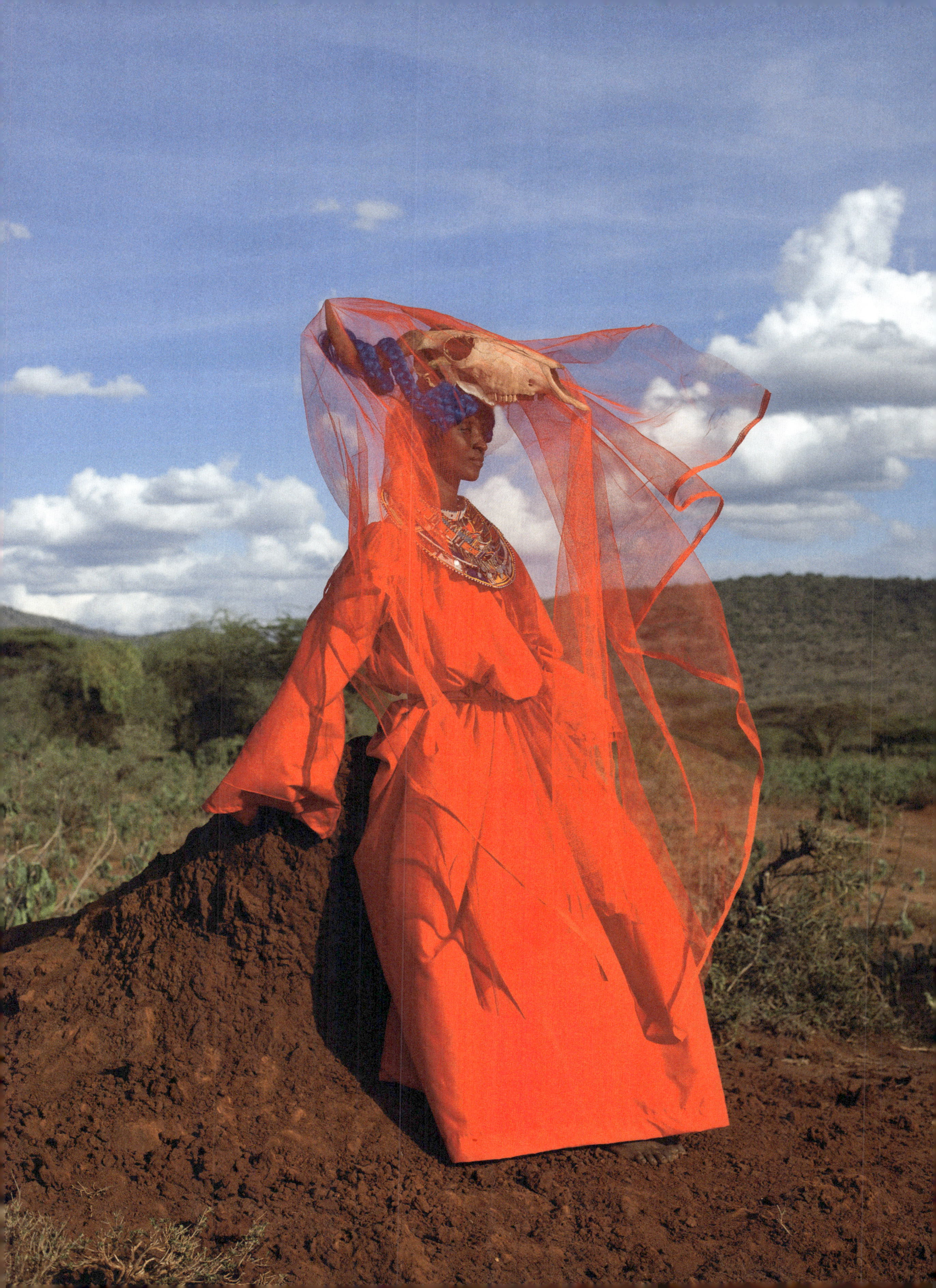

Ruth Moige

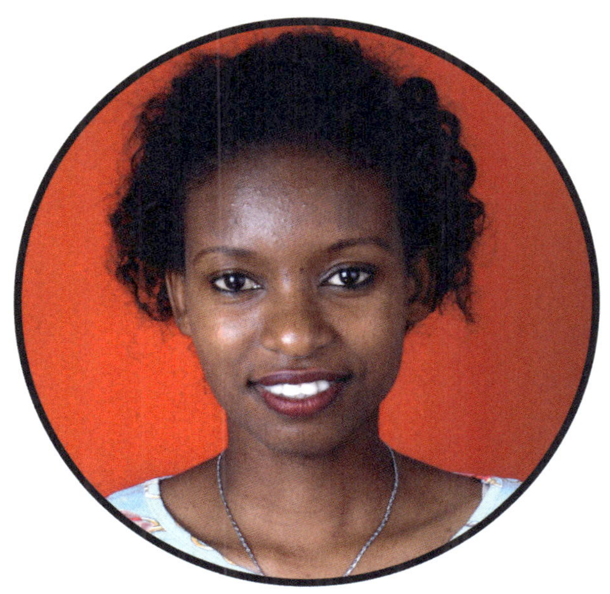

Grew up in: Nairobi (Rongai)

Age: 21

Silky hair and not bravery or grit, tan coloured skin and not vivid ethnocultutal expression; these are the things that first drew Ruth Moige to the Maa people. Growing up in Ongata Rongai, a Maasai enclave just outside of Nairobi, Ruth was anaesthetised at an early age to the charms of Maa culture, so all that was left was just the physical form. A form which she continues to fetishise. 'They just make such beautiful babies. I must find myself a Maasai husband,' she says coyly. The 20-year-old student of photography aims to shift focus from the banal conversation surrounding the cultural wealth of the Maasai to a rendition of their genetic aesthetic and its preservation through offspring. While there have not been any real signs of a Maasai husband in her future, she does admit to having a crush on some unsuspecting gentleman. May the odds be ever in her favour.

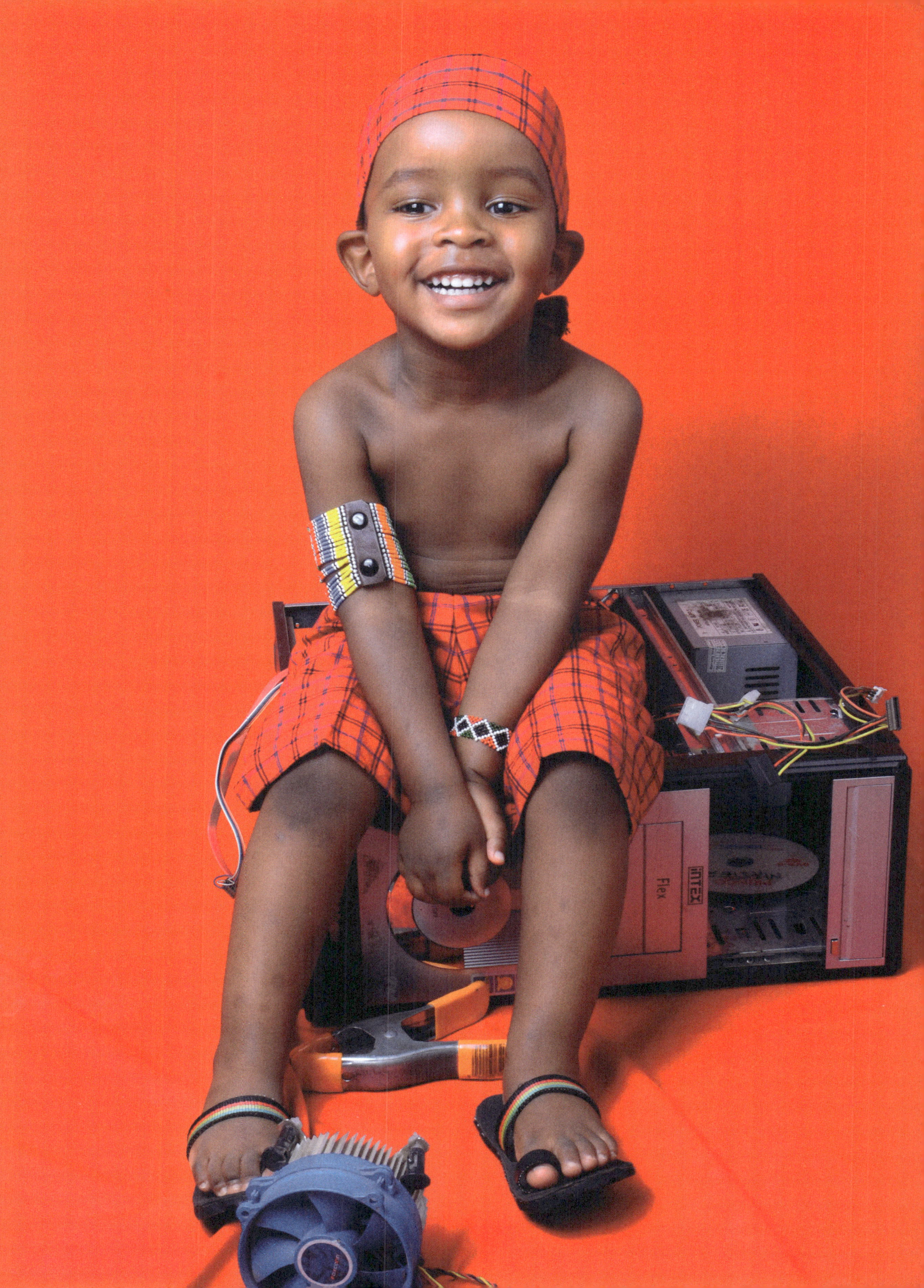
intex
Flex

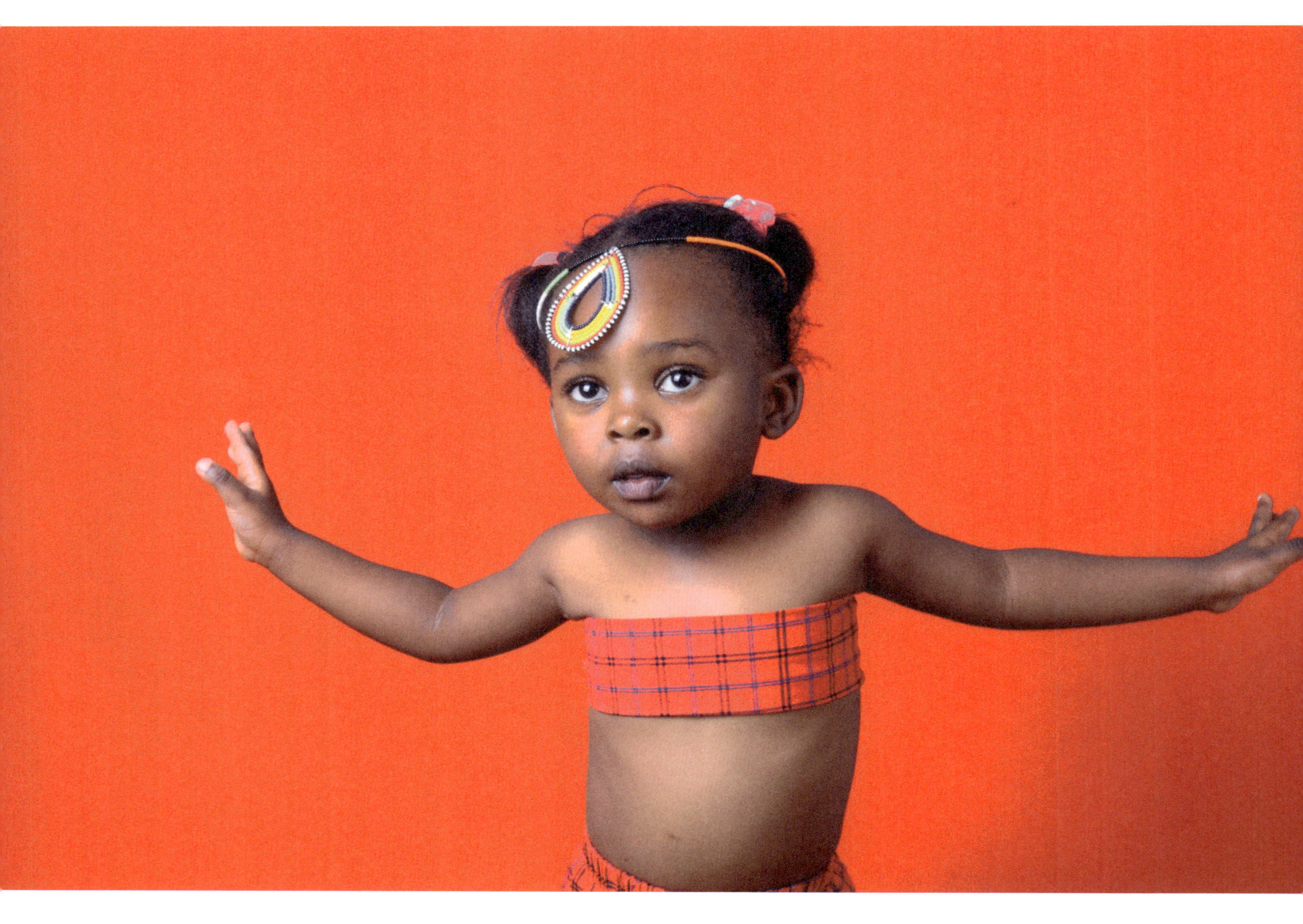

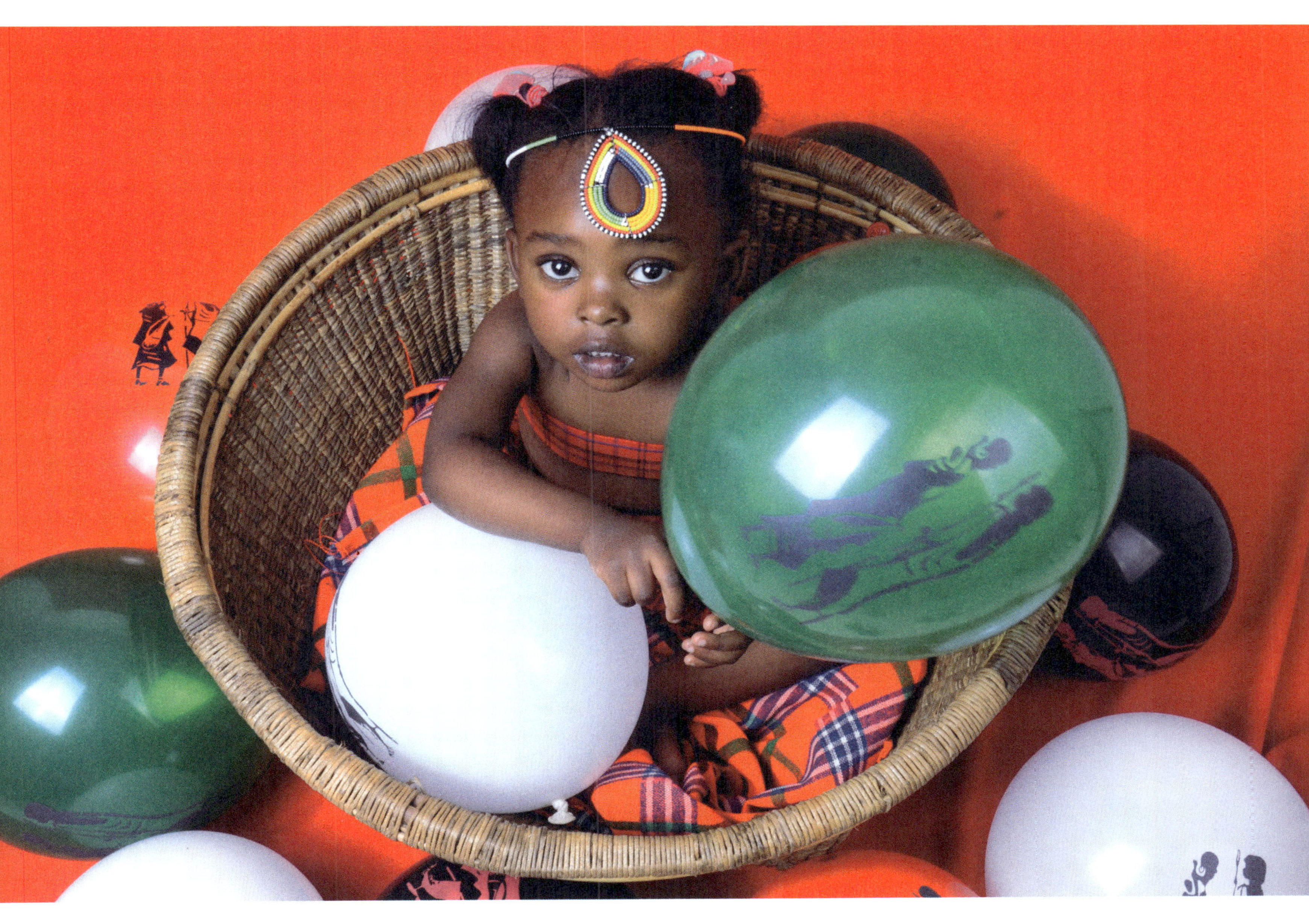

Joel Lukhovi

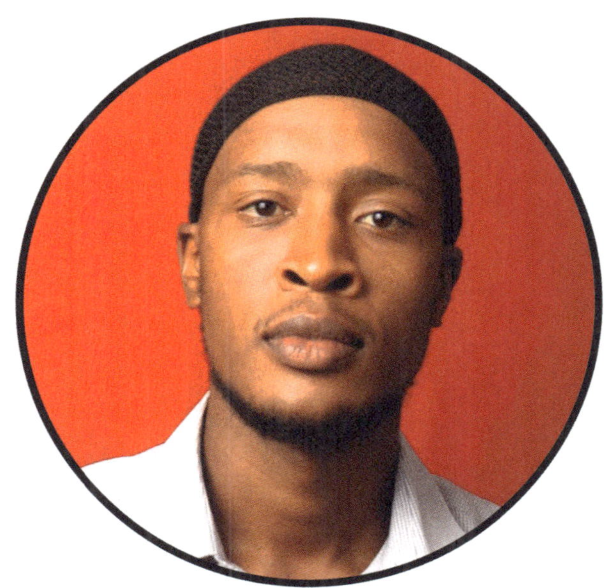

Grew up in: Nairobi

Age: 30

Engineers and architects have a long history of dipping their toes in the pond of photography and taking to it famously. Joel Lukhovi is the perfect exemplification of what happens when a passion for photography marries a background in engineering. He sees beauty where many do not; in the texture of a wall, the patterns of roofing or the asymmetry in a fence of twigs. Joel who has lived and worked among the Maasai investigates with his camera lens the meanings of spaces and their significance to them. Using the black and white technique to cancel out noise and bring focus to his subjects, he represents the culture of the Maa people in ways uncommon to his peers.

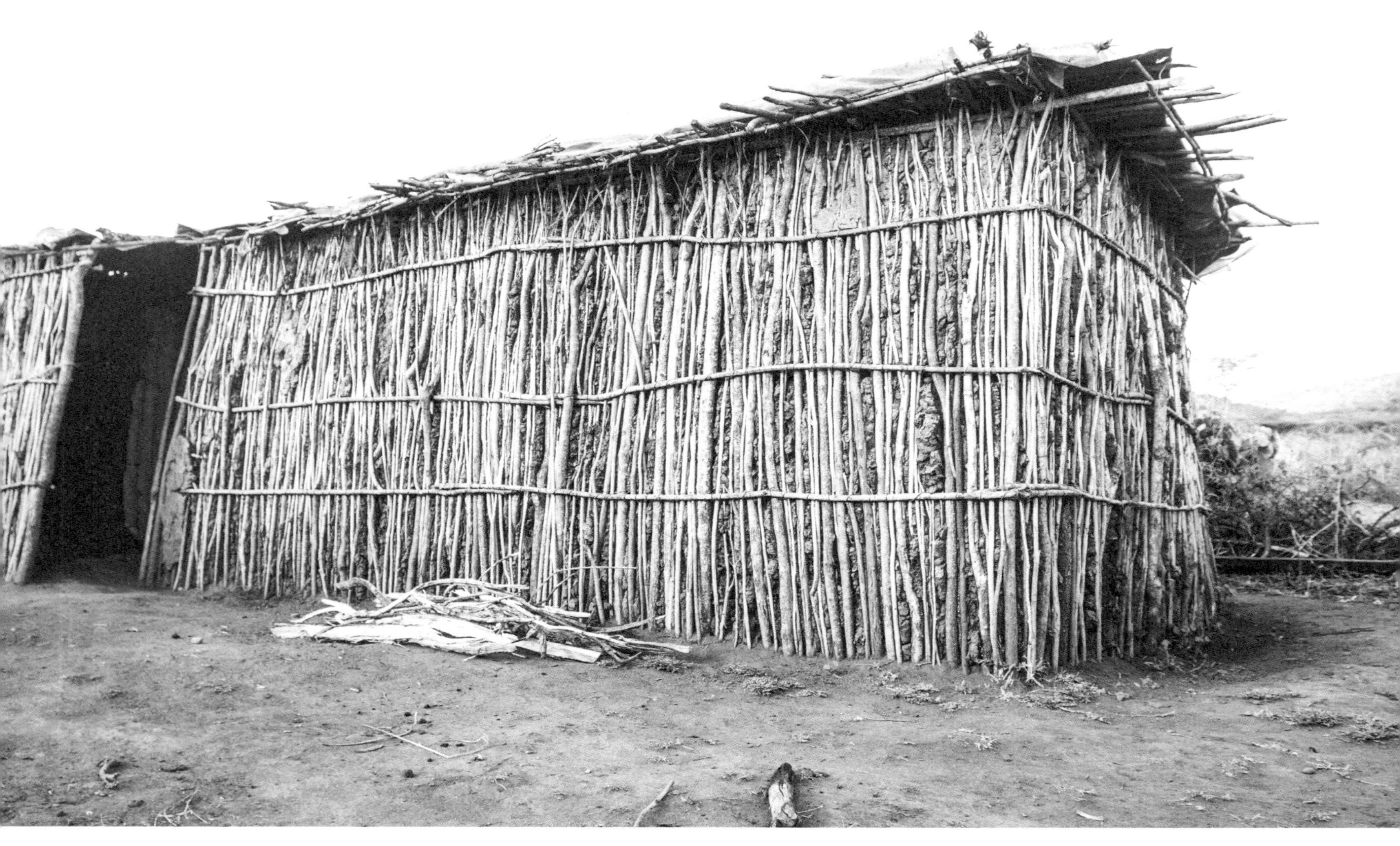

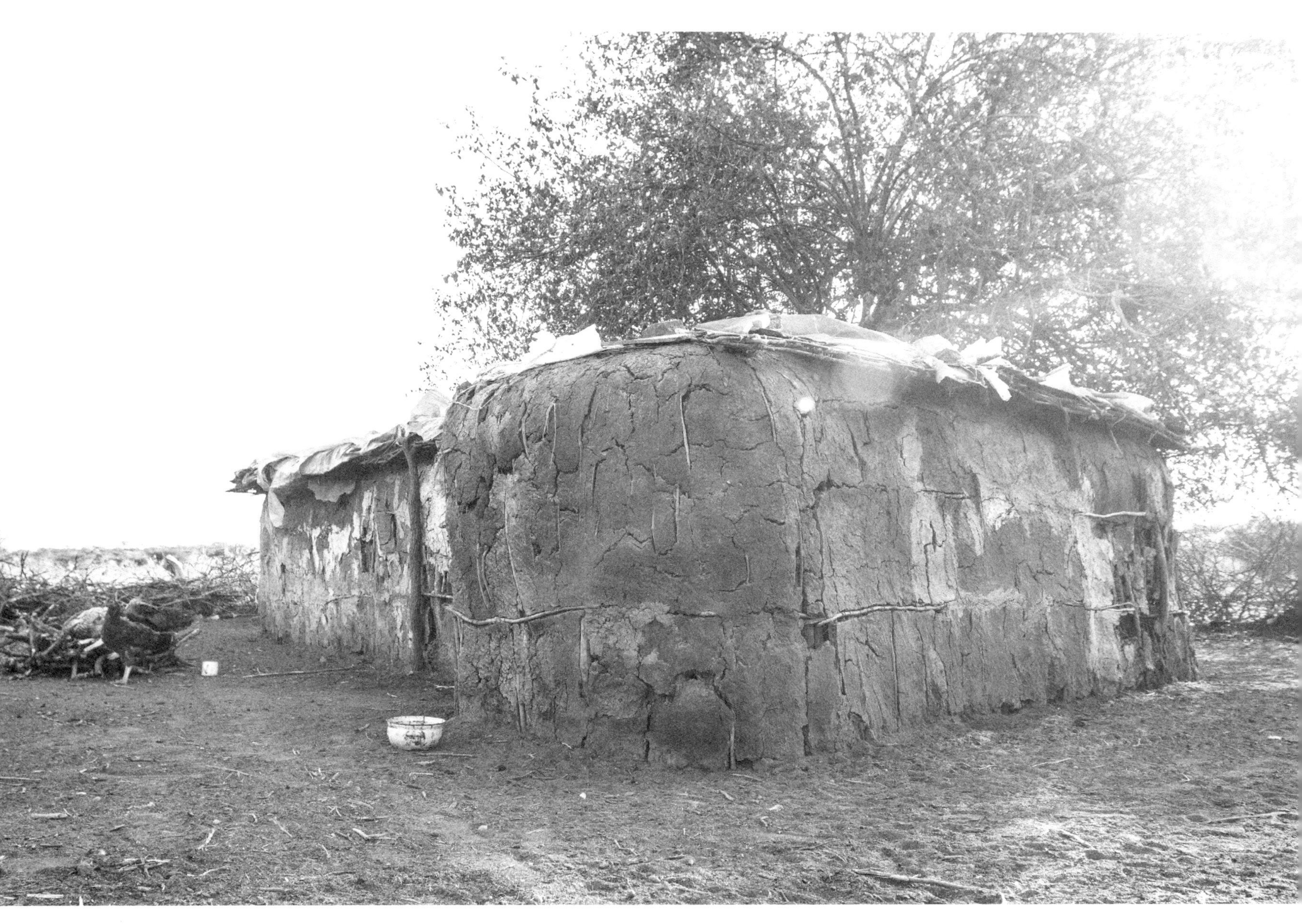

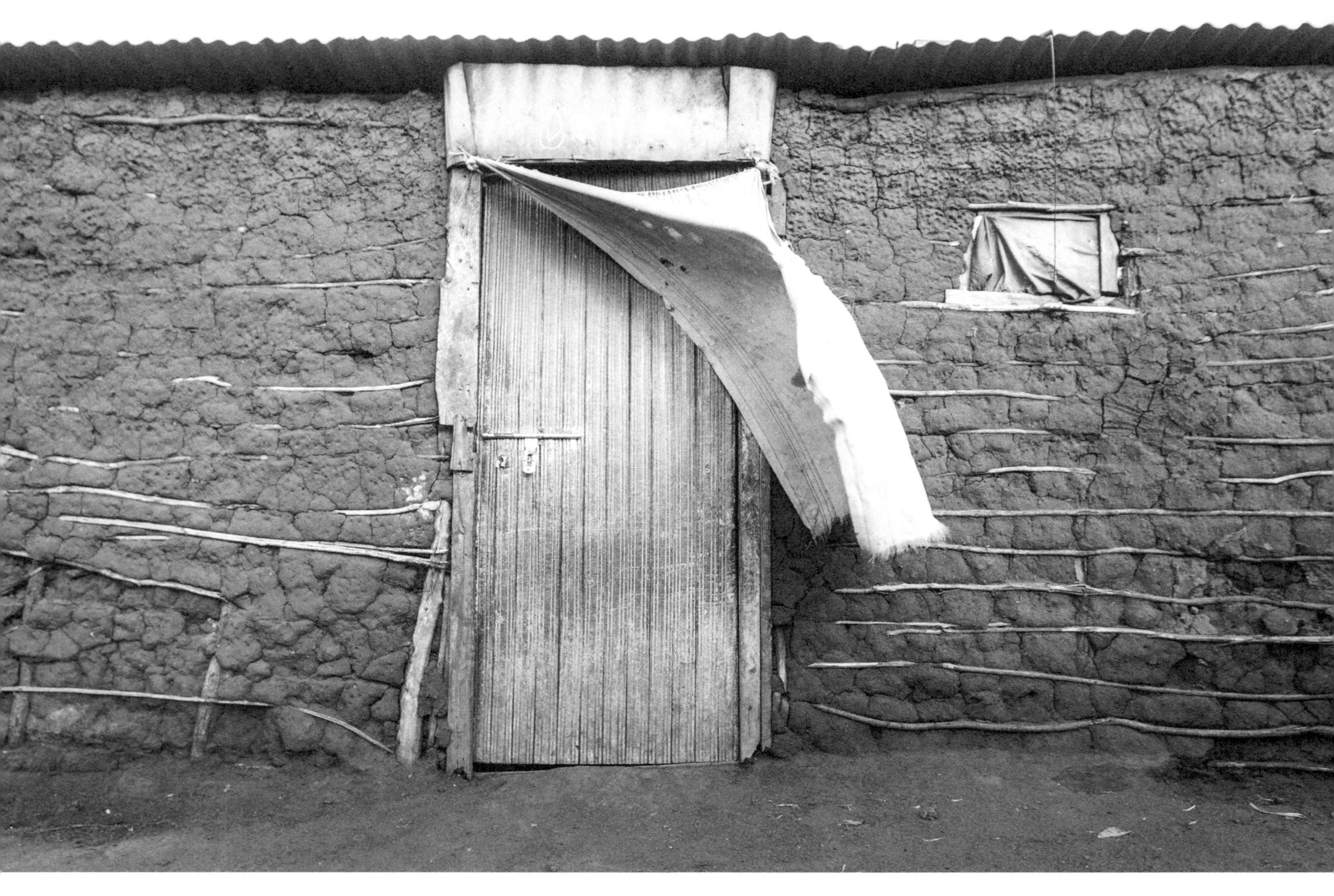

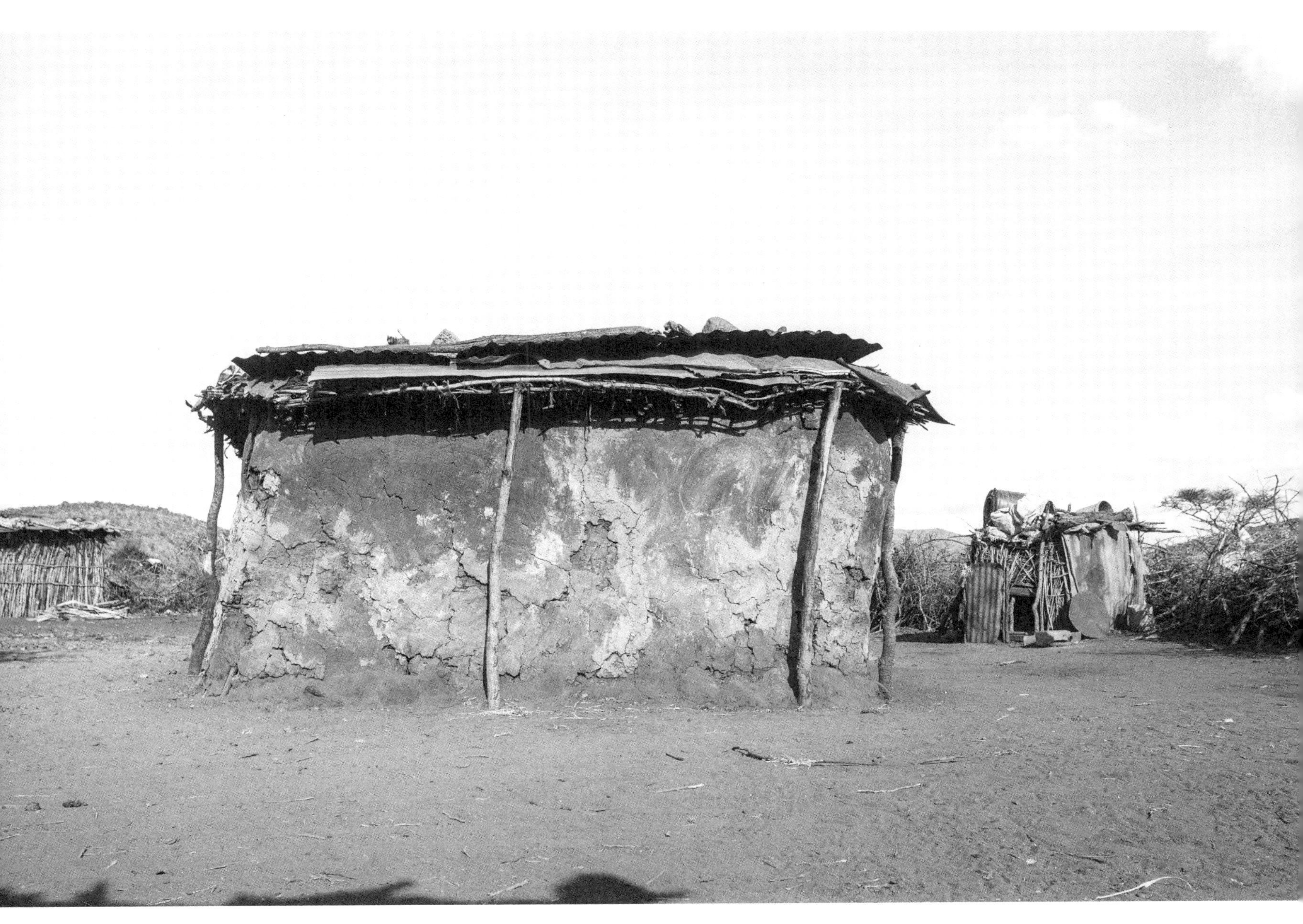

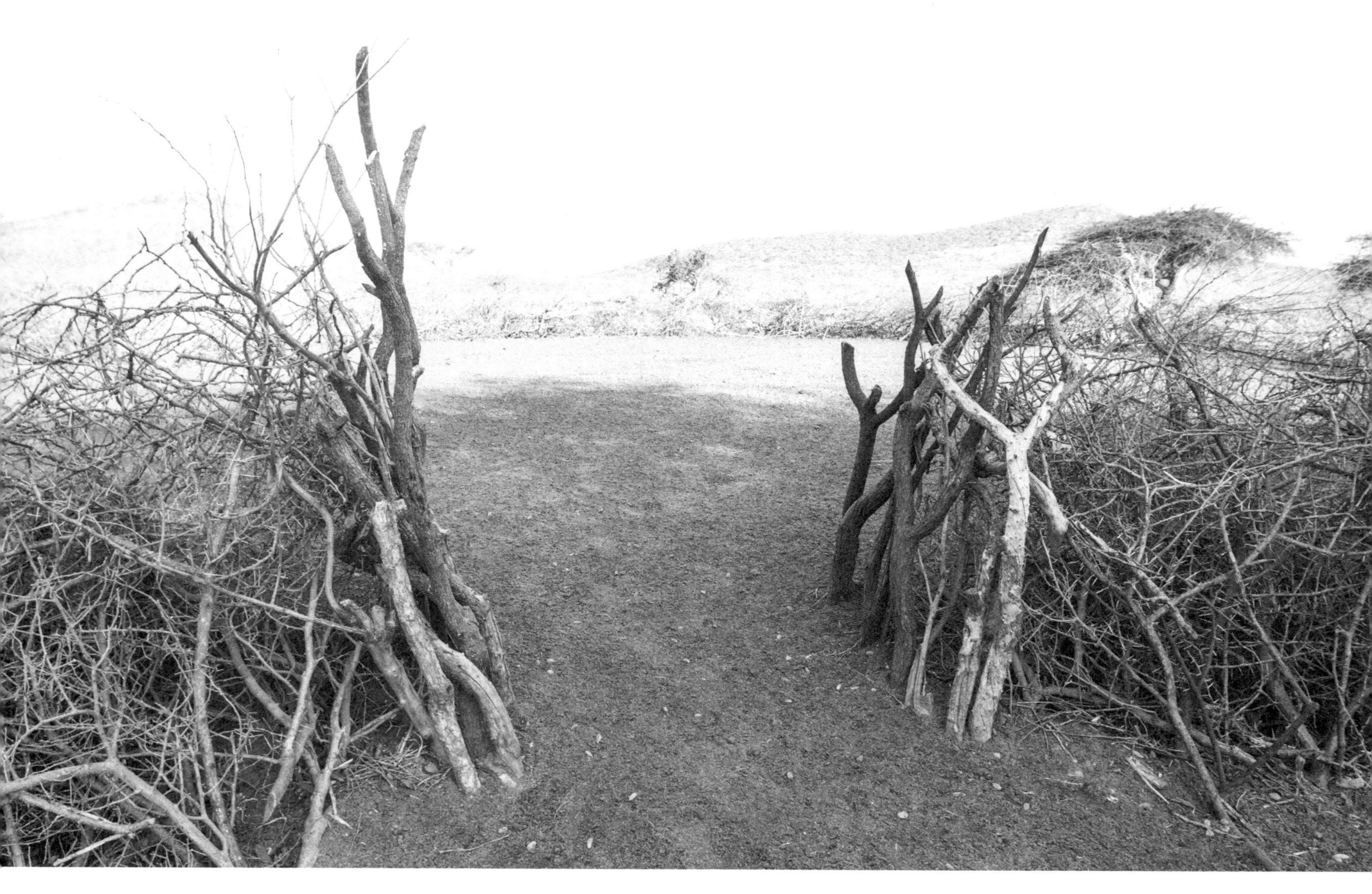

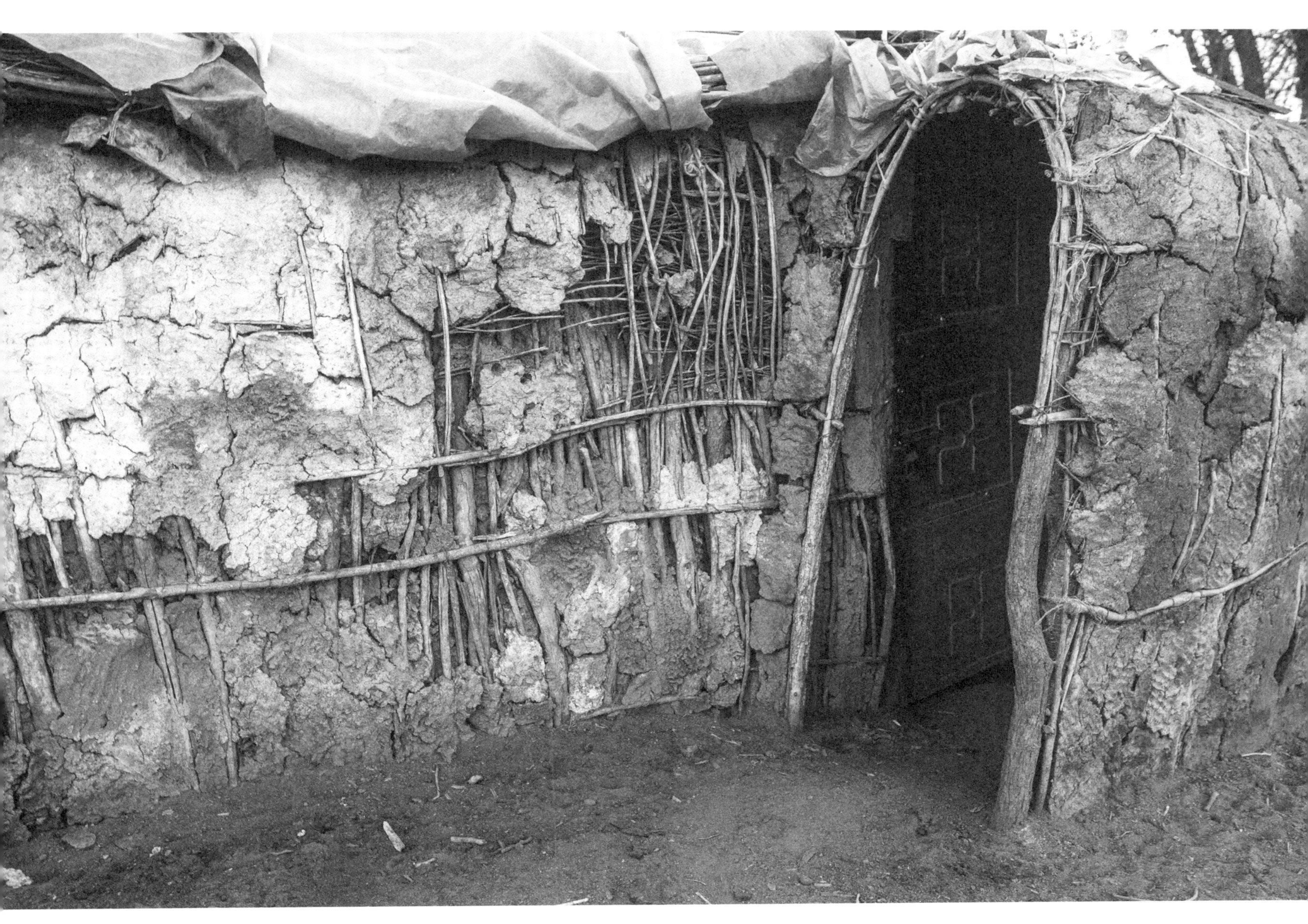

Mercy Billy

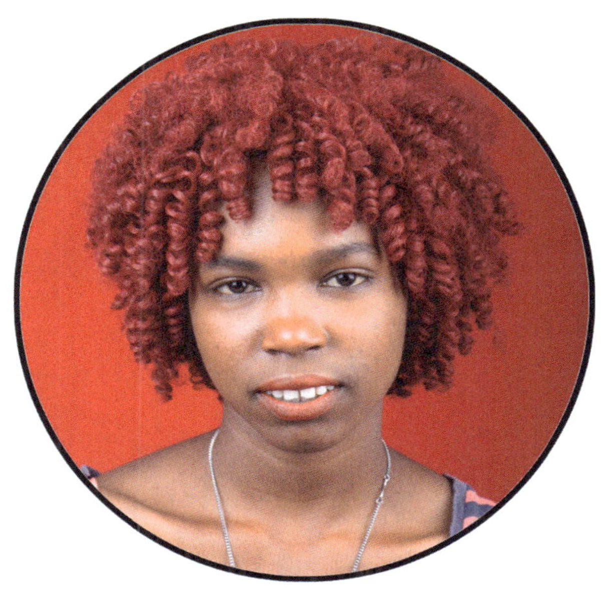

Grew up in: Kiambu
Age: 21

Having only ever known the Maasai to be good for work as security guards because of their reputation as ferocious fighters, Mercy Billy was surprised to meet one who was of all things, a pilot! She now acknowledges that the Maa of today are a multifaceted people whose sheer determination has seen them transcend the mischaracterisation imposed on them unfairly by public opinion.

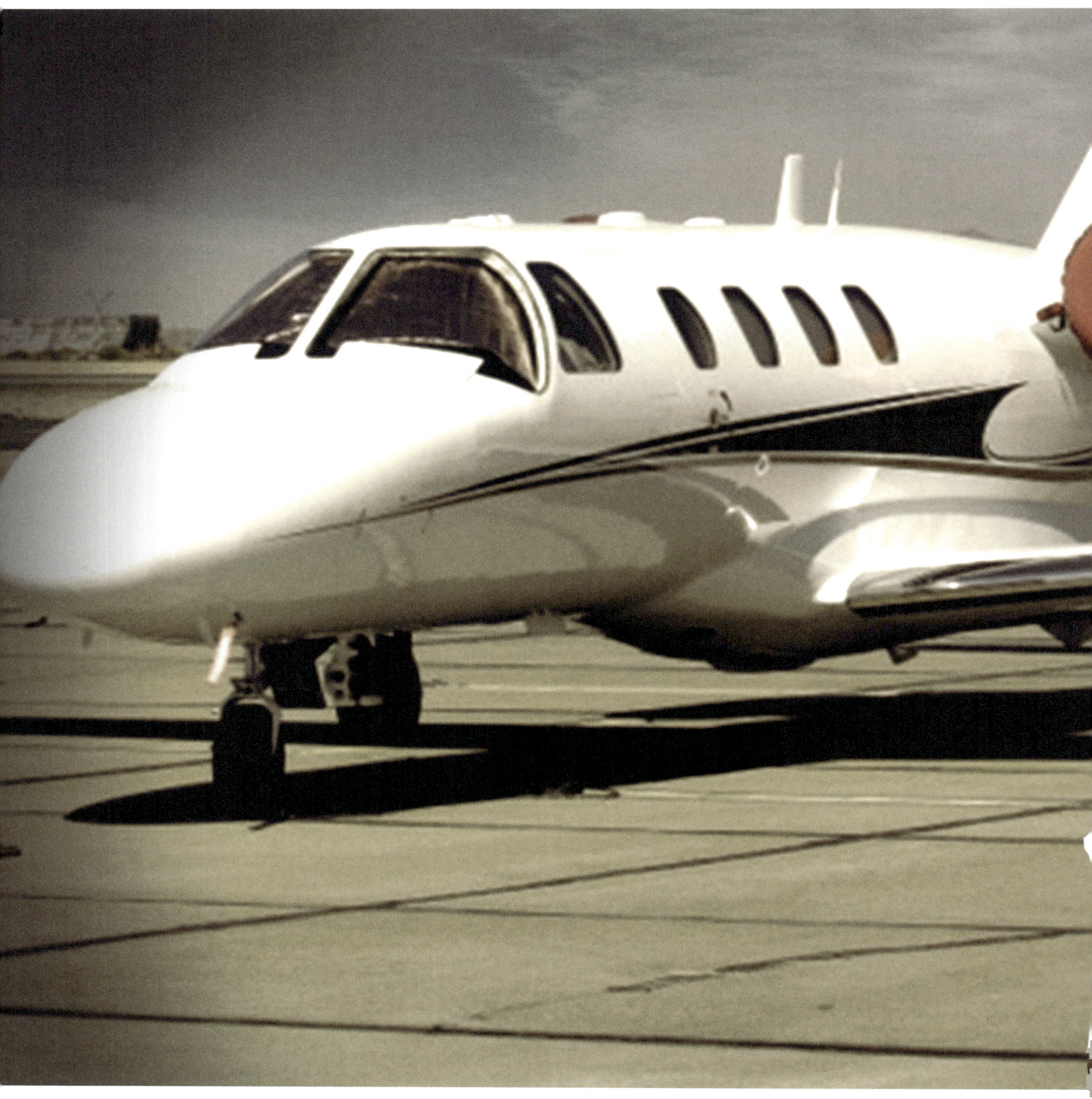

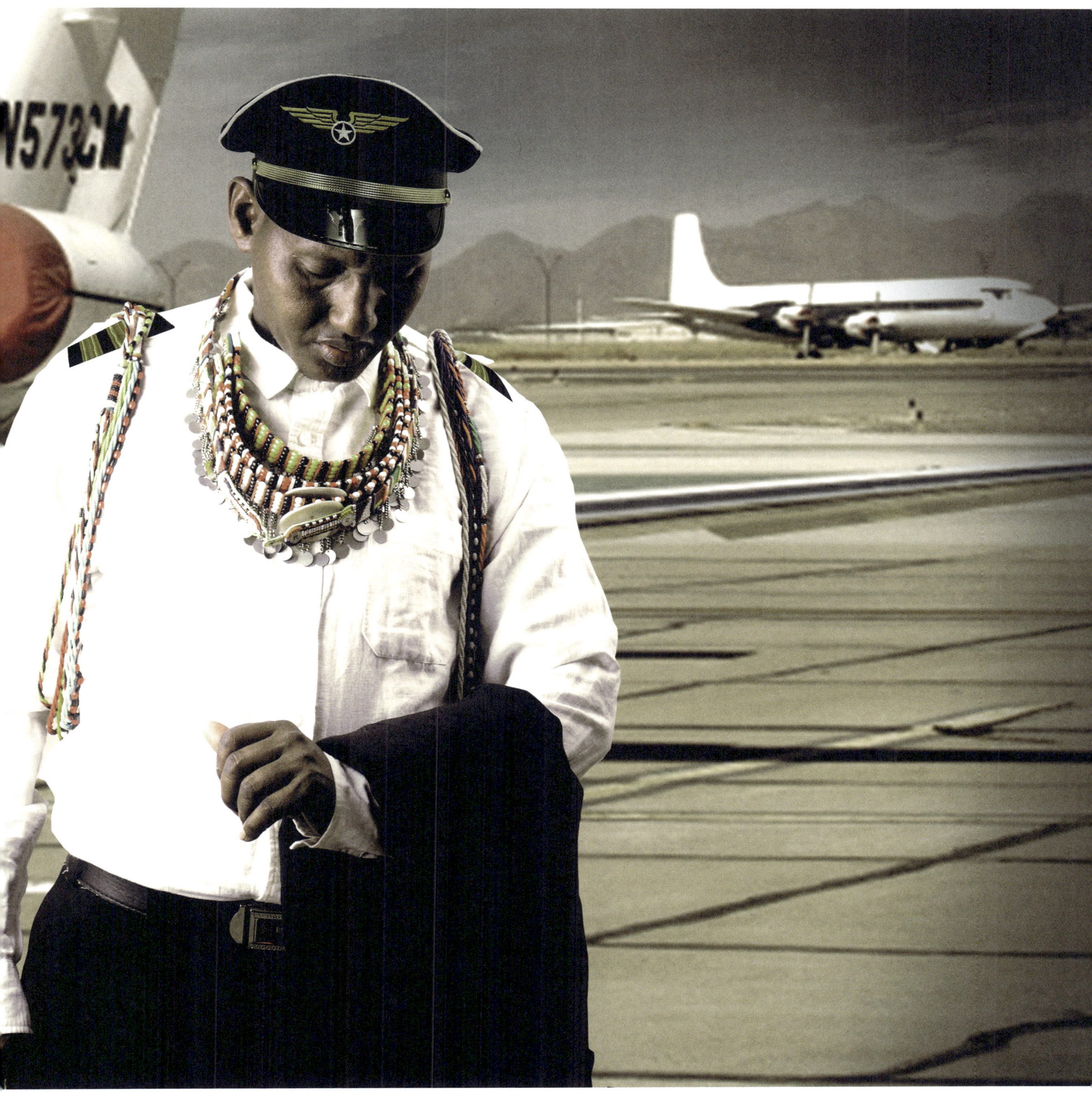
N573CM

Allan Mwangi

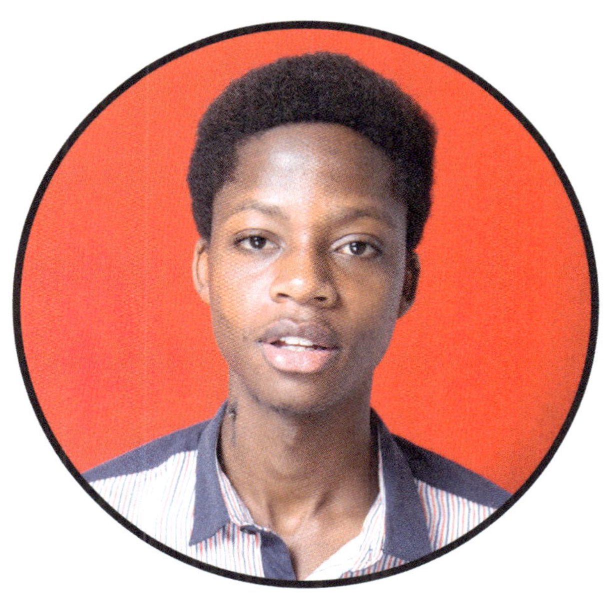

Grew up in: Nakuru

Age: 19

Called the 'War Photographer' by his friends and family because of his attraction to high stress environments, this 19-year-old aims to challenge the existing perceptions of the Maasai. He dislikes that the portrayal of Maa men is almost always as small bodied men leaning on sticks and watching over herd of cattle so he set out to find bulky sportsmen who participate in sports reserved for an elite club which the Maasai have been locked out of for generations.

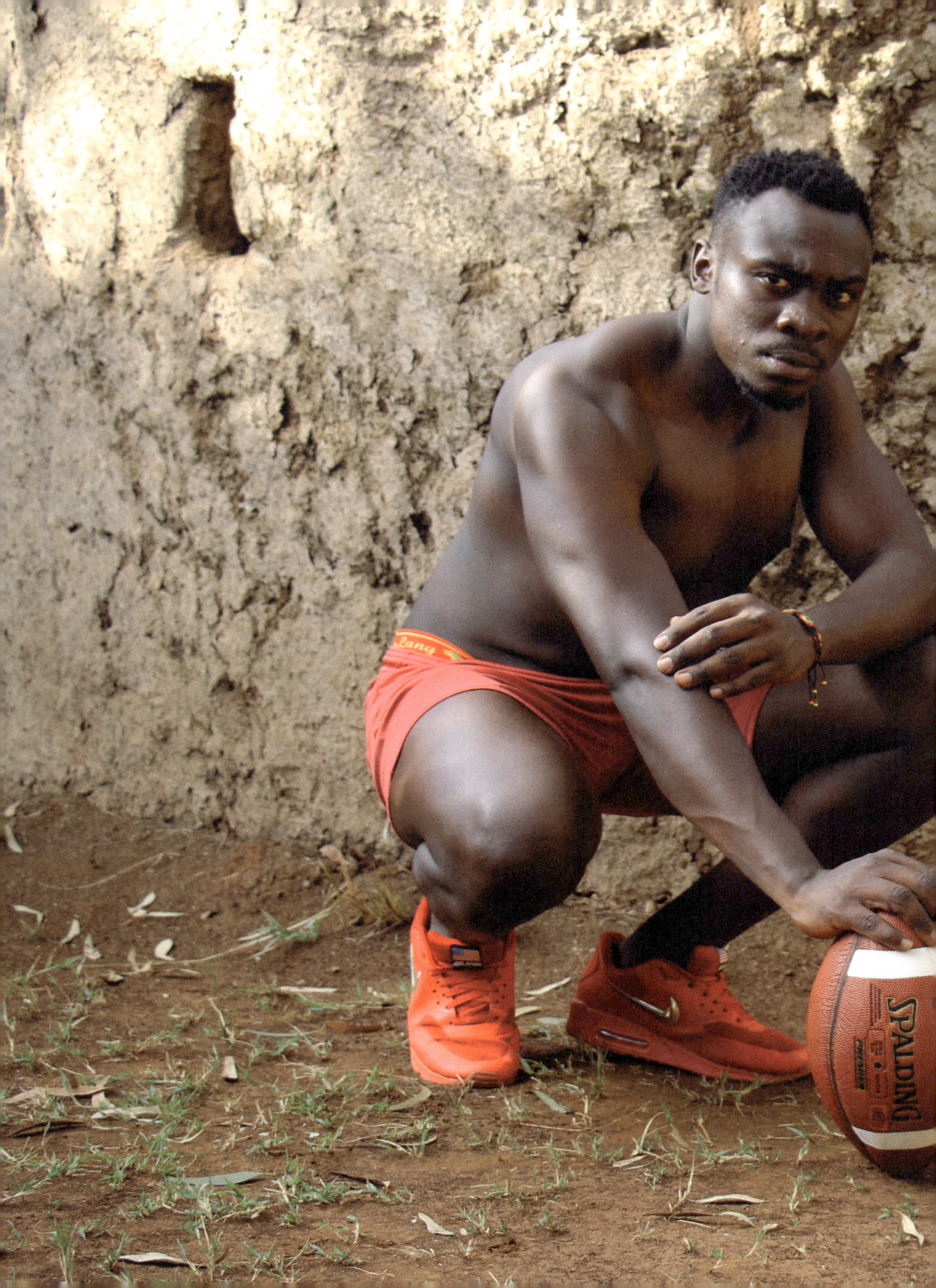
SPALDING

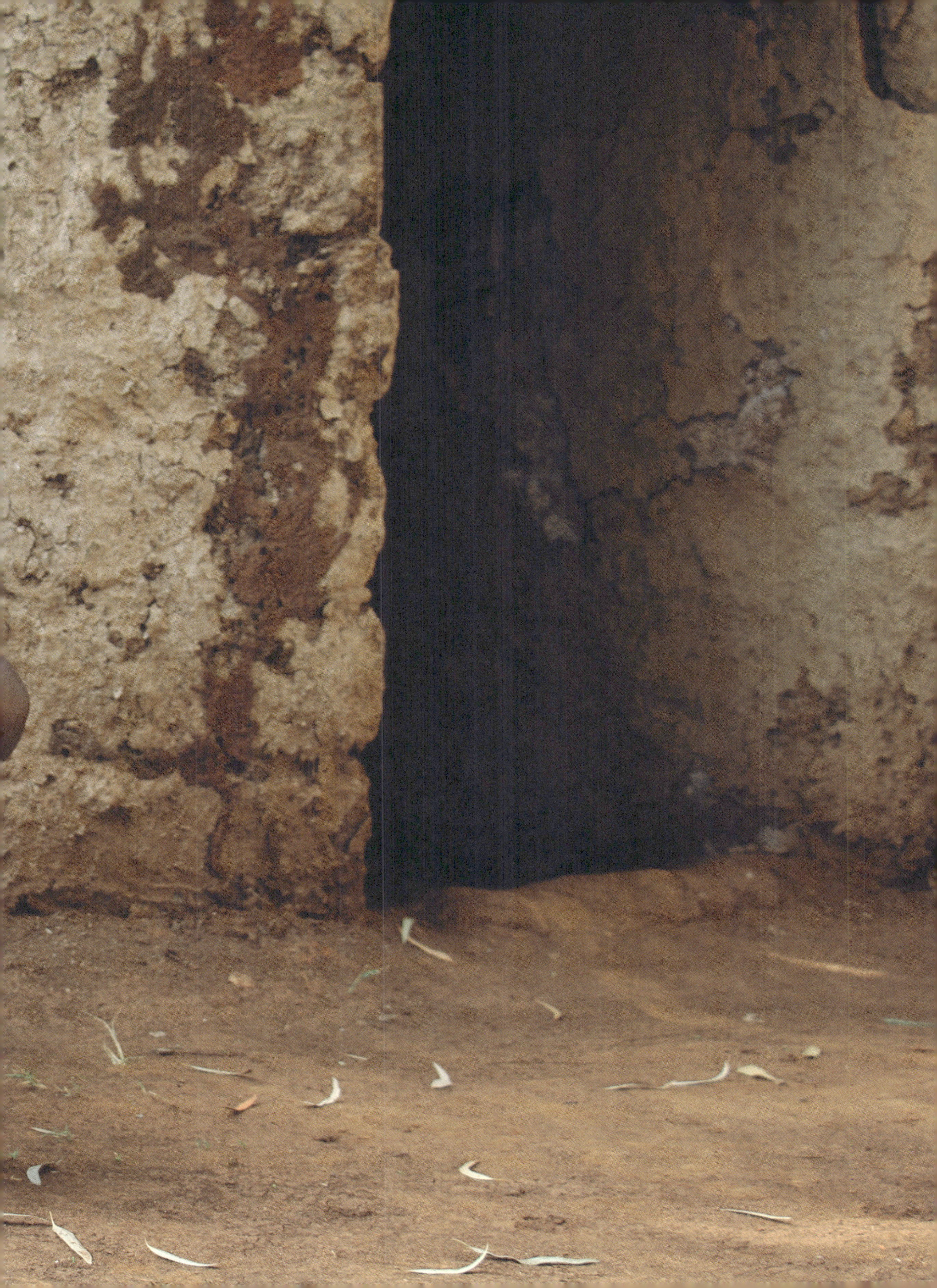

June Odiembo

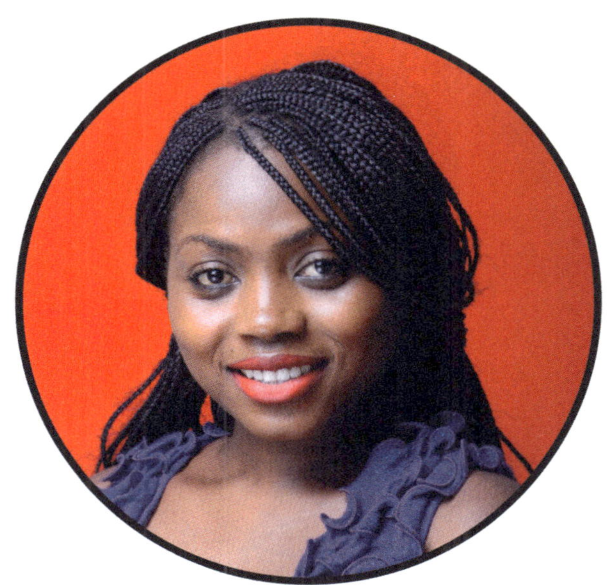

Grew up in: Nairobi
Age: 22

June Odiembo fits the heteronormative mould of a 'normal' girl child raised in a semi-conservative family. She has never indulged in or desired sexual activity seen as deviant by the society which designed and informed her moral code. A code that doesn't abide 'unconventional' manifestations of sexuality. But as with most High School encounters, she met with a conundrum which required for her to choose between an allegiance to the code and tolerance of that which threatened it. She chose the latter, when a Maasai schoolmate of hers disclosed that she was a lesbian. The bleakness being gay in a society which dehumanises sexual minorities spoke to June's humanity. She now dedicates her craft to growing the visibility of these marginalised communities. In what is a rebuke of the status quo, June captures scenes which provoke and sensitise audiences to the fact that love indeed reigns supreme.

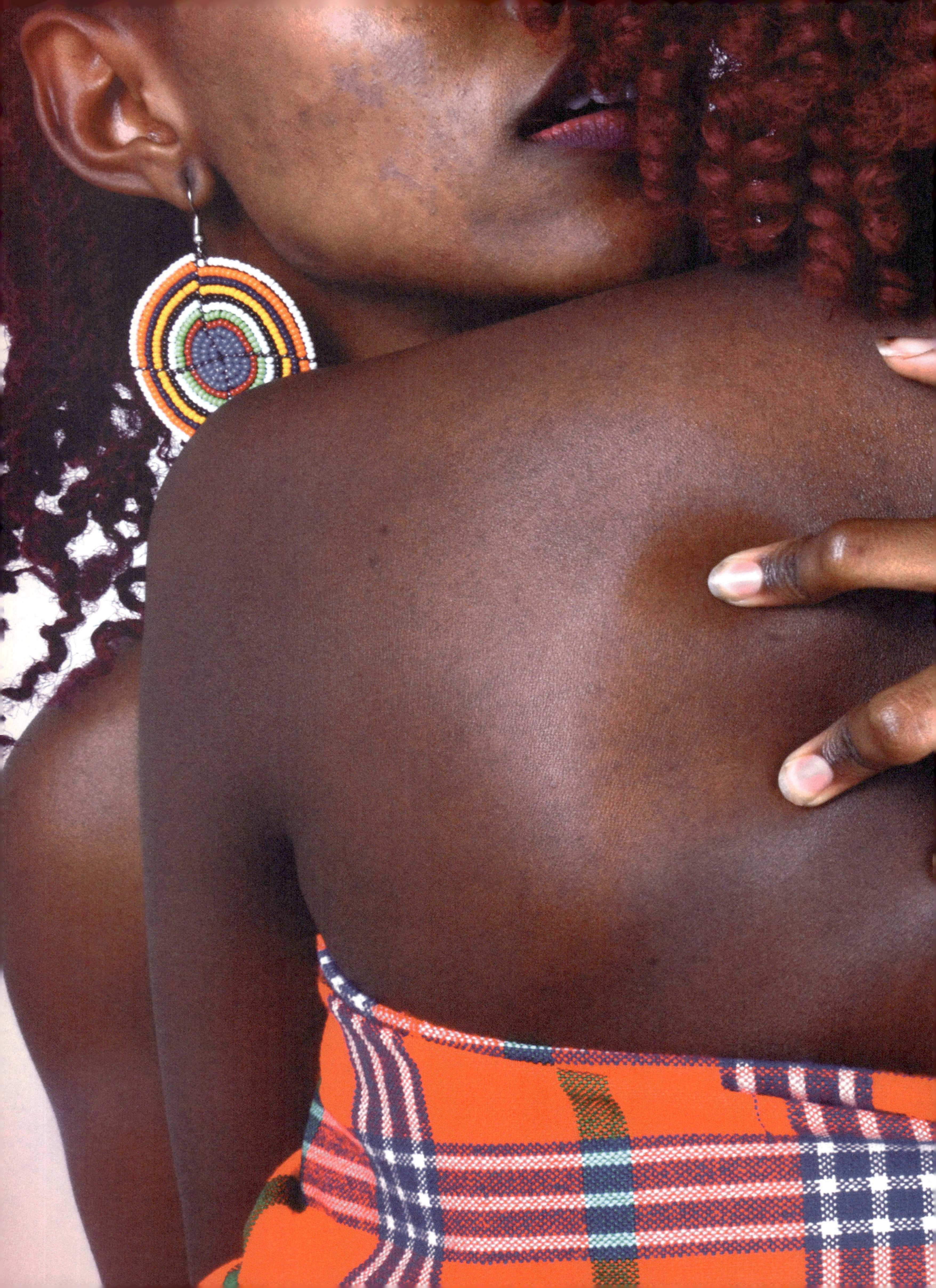

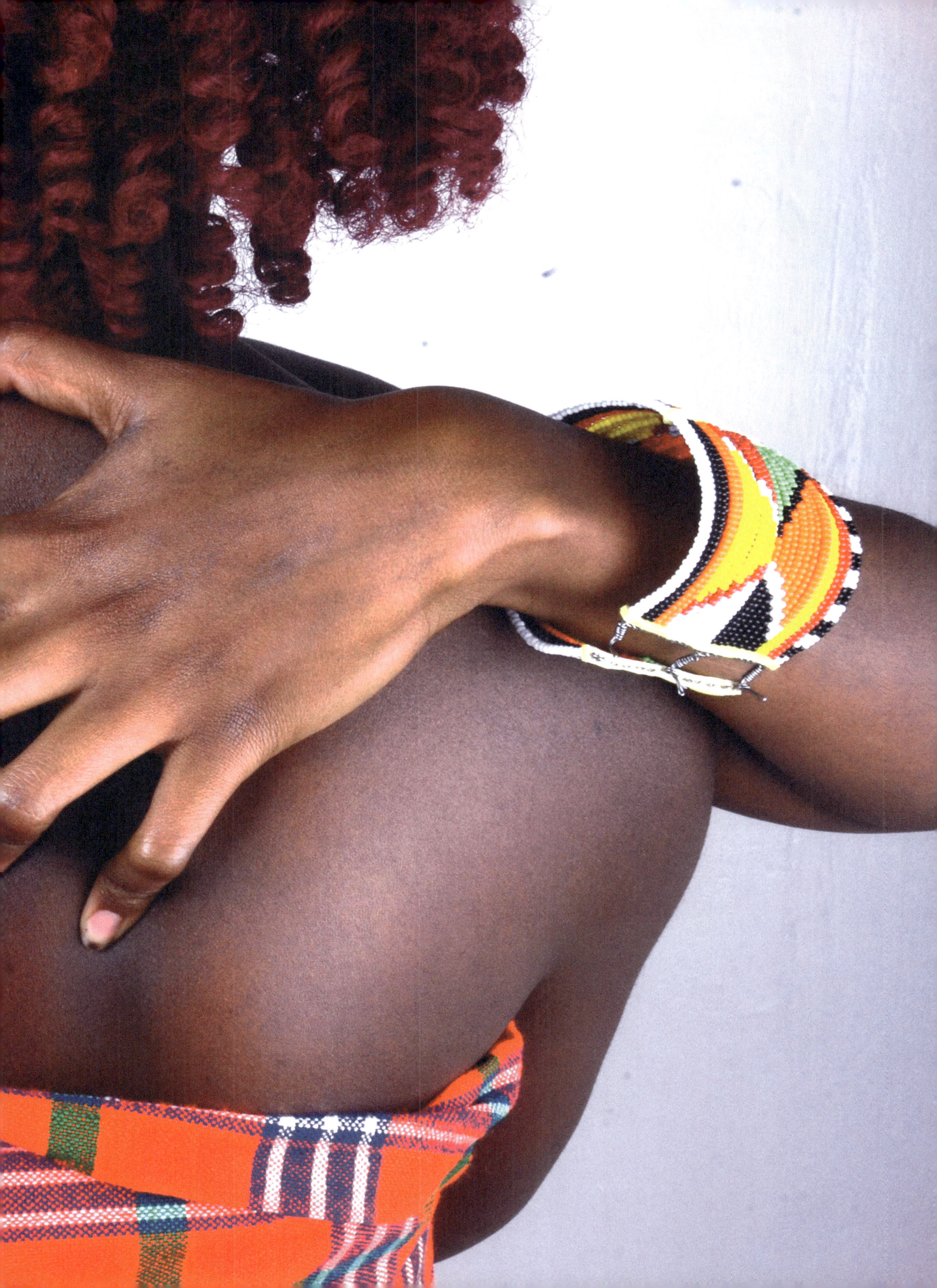

Perrine Philomeen

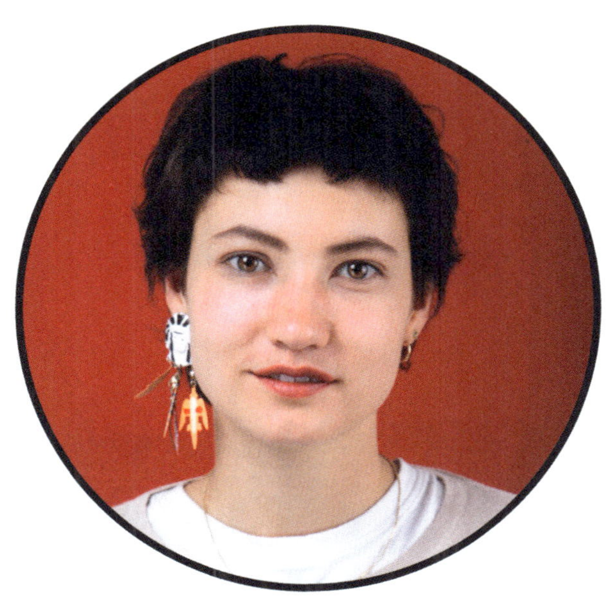

Grew up in: Rotterdam, the Netherlands

Age: 24

(in collaboration with Godlisten Meshack)

Dutch student of fashion design and collaborative creator of avant-garde garments Perrine Philomeen knew nothing about the Maa people beyond their dress when she met She was therefore stunned to discover Godlisten who at face could pass for any other African male going about their business in a city that has little patience for those who do not conform to its standard. Pondering the question of what a future for the Maasai people would look like, Perrine's mind wandered to a place of great amusement. She creates a post-apocalyptic world where the human race with the exception of the Maa people is completely wiped off the face of the planet. Having to adapt to the hostile air which is choking with poisonous elements, the remaining Maasai must transform the way the dress to ensure their survival.

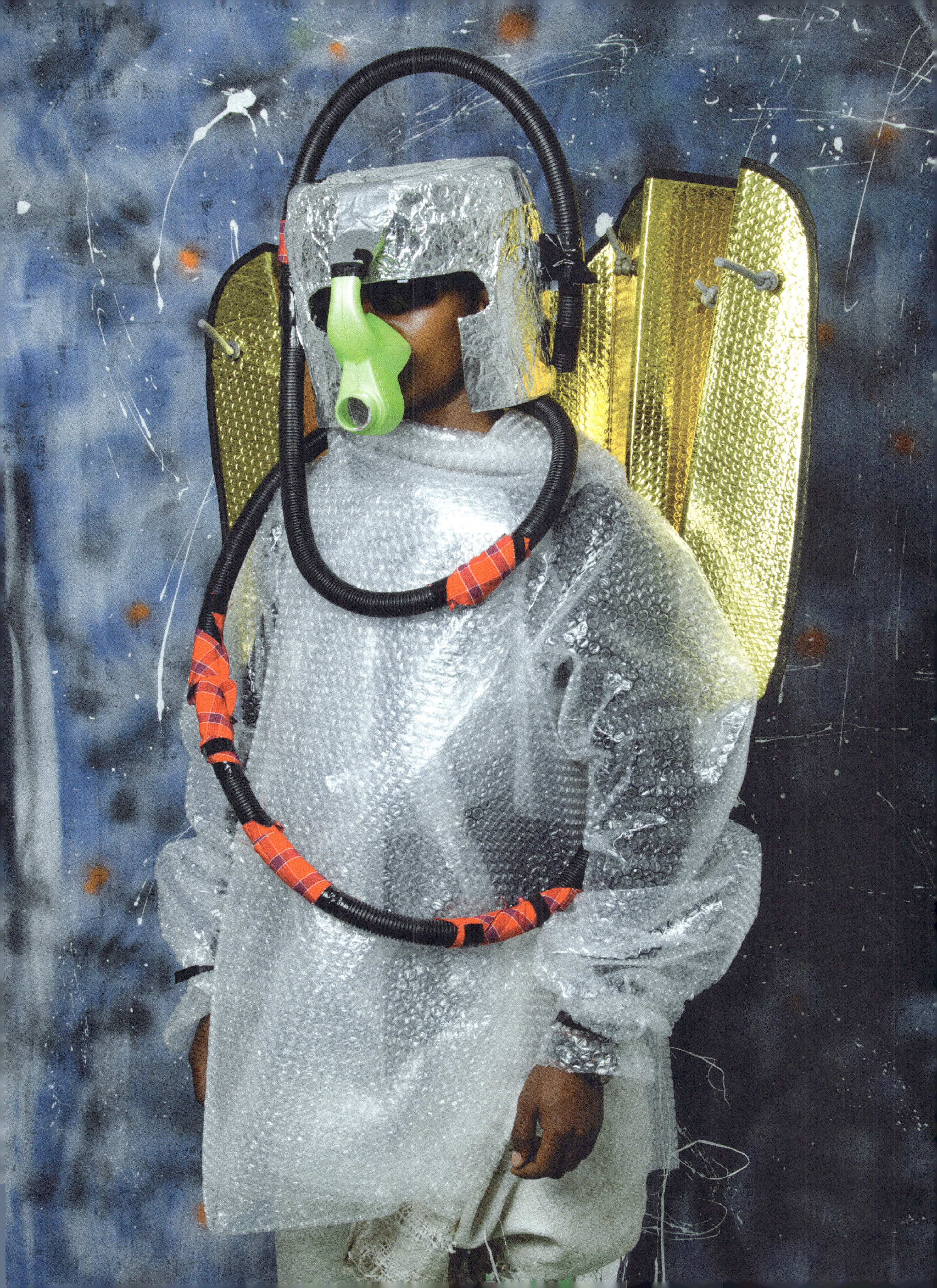

Joshua Piri

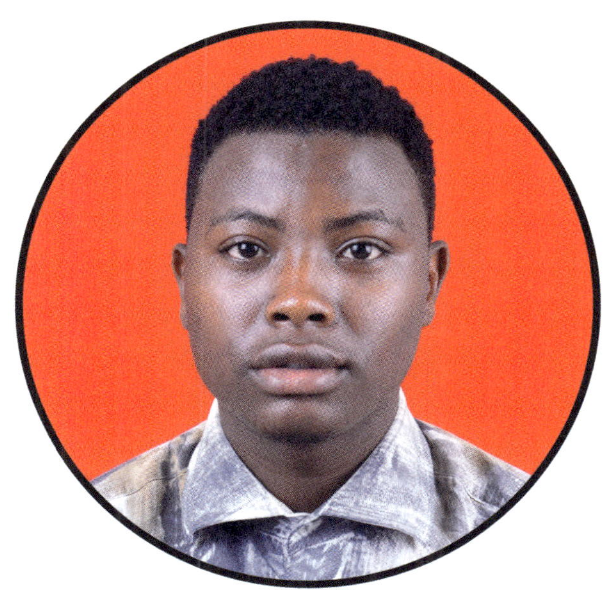

Grew up in: Kinango, Kwale County
Age: 20

Excited by the advancement of the marriage rites among the Maasai people from the ways of the past to more contemporary arrangements, Joshua Piri captures the integration of cultural Maasai elements and modern rites of marriage through quirky kaleidoscopic images. Owing to a long history of forced and arranged marriages influenced heavily by ancient tradition, weddings where the bride played an active role in planning are a fairly novel activity among the Maa people. The Western import of white weddings is also a new trend which Joshua rarely ever saw in his days growing up in in the coastal county of Kwale in Kenya where most Maasai weddings adhered to the dictates of tradition.

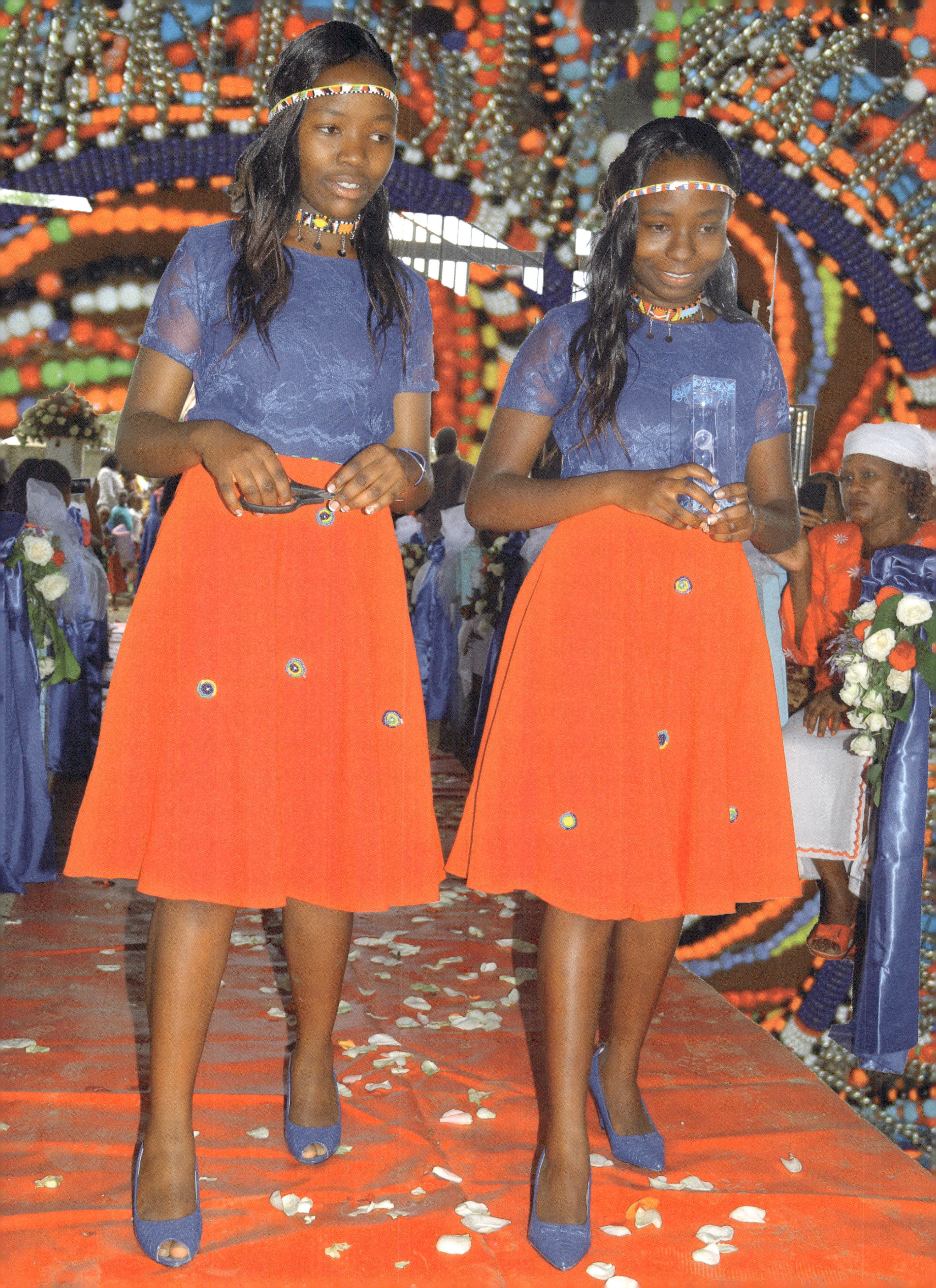

Cyrus Mugo

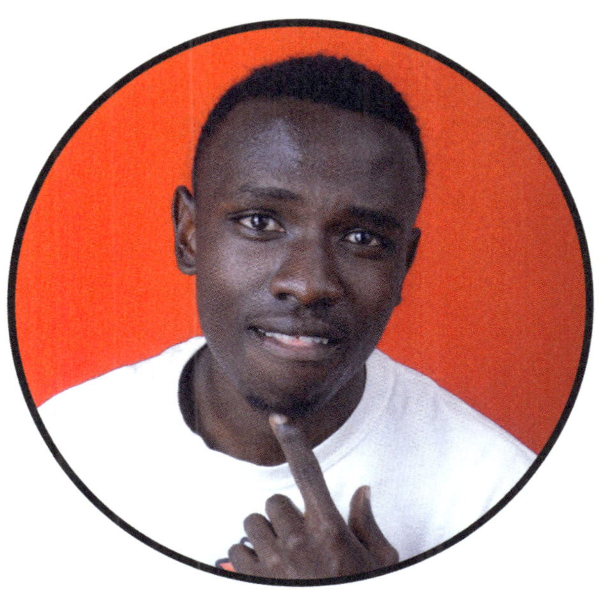

Grew up in: Nakuro
Age: 21

Cyrus Mugo's depictions of the Maasai trying to navigate the urban spaces within which they operate are relatable and allow for the formerly misguided to readjust their attitudes towards them and start seeing them as ordinary members of the populace and not some exotic creatures of mystique. He expresses the need for the Maasai to integrate themselves into modern society with powerful images of a Maasai man in a barber's chair as if waiting to undergo an initiation ritual. With every hair that falls from his head, the subject leaves a little of his old self behind. Among the electronic equipment and western style dressed people in the barber shop, his Maasai 'shuka' sticks out, but as the barber works his head, he gets closer and closer to reaching the status of modernity that society demands of him.

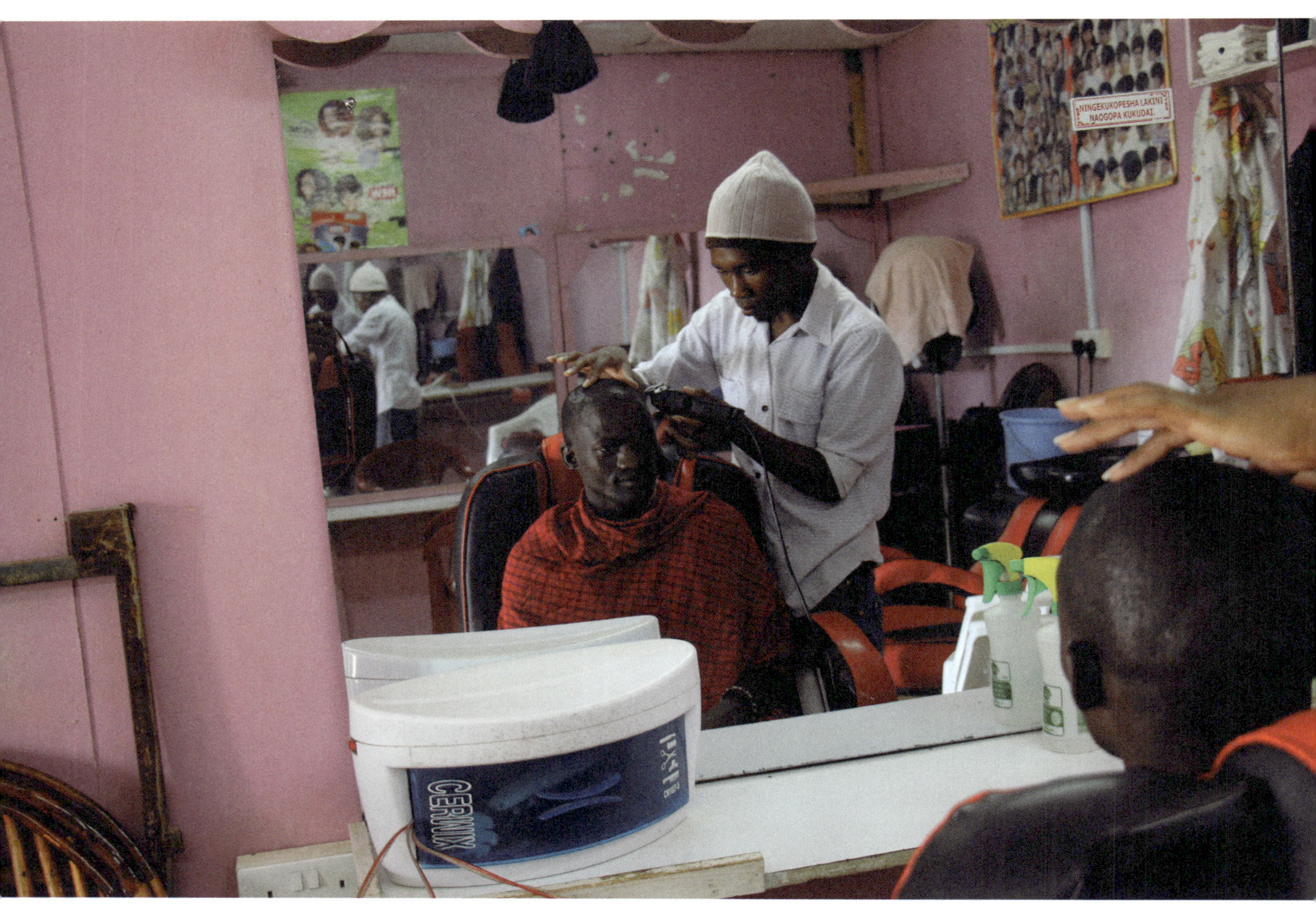
NINGEKUKOPESHA LAKINI
NAOGOPA KUKUDAI.

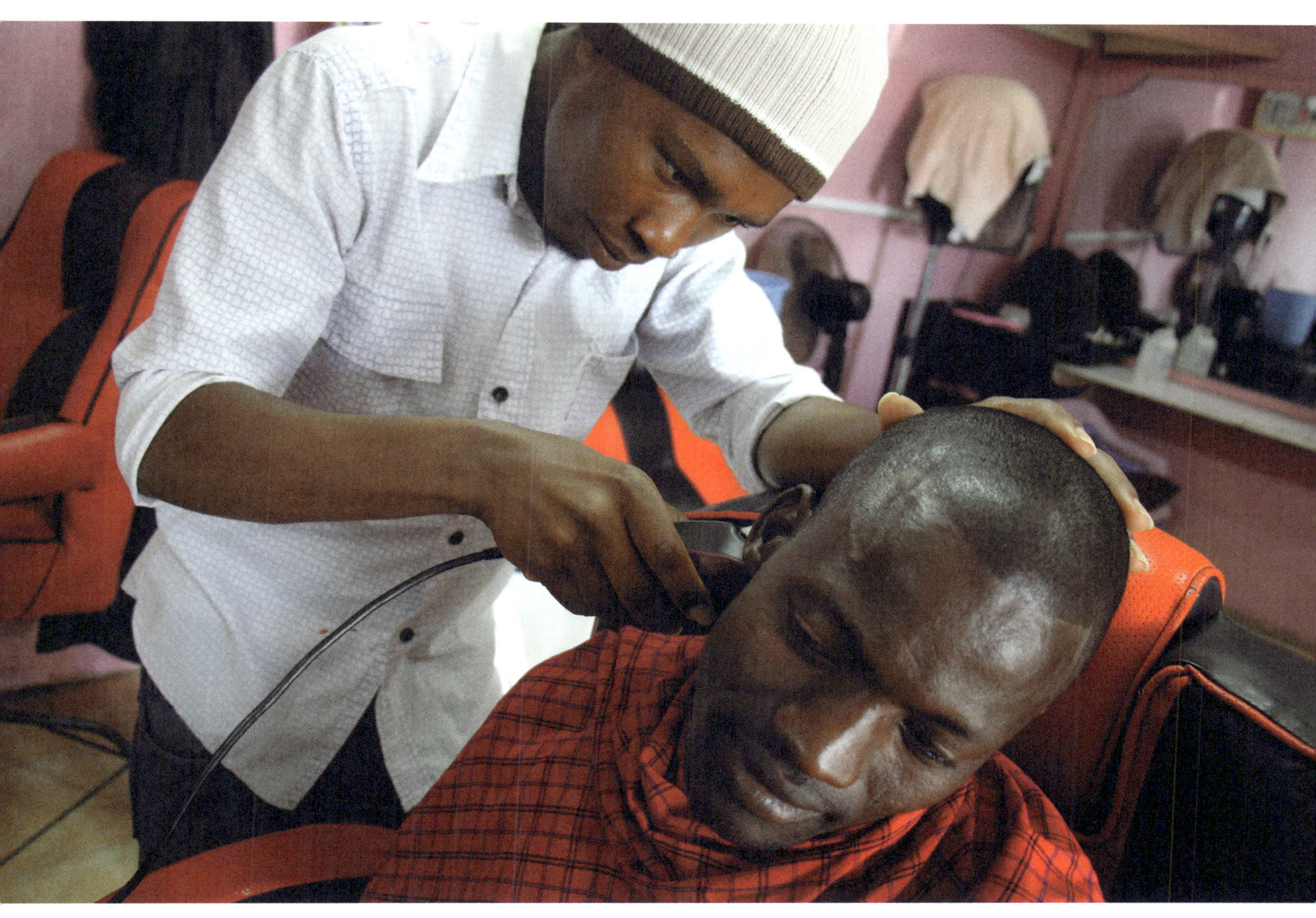

Lotte Van Eijk

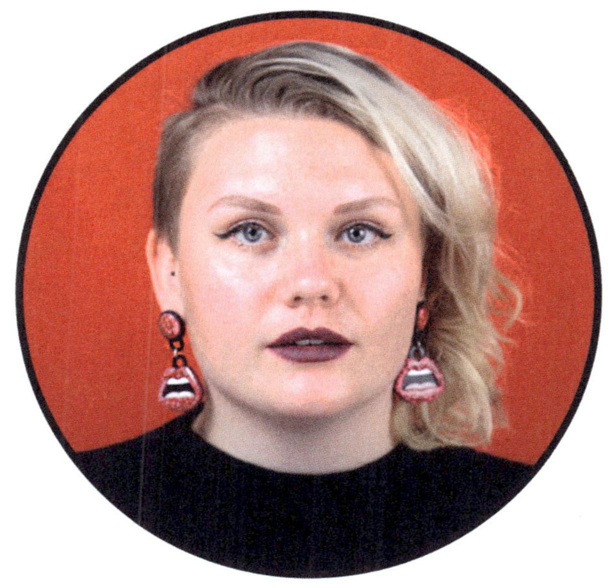

Grew up in: Rotterdam
Age: 20

Lotte Van Eijk's Dutch outsider eyes present an interesting outlook. A big girl who loves her form, Lotte has only ever known the Maasai as a bunch of primitive folk from the continent of wonders featured in travelogues. She believed that the female body was in Africa, only as desirable as its breadth and took this opportunity to investigate standards of female beauty among the Maa. It surprised her to learn that the voluptuous female form is now a source of ridicule owing largely to the pervasiveness of Hollywood culture amongst modern Maasai females. But her assumptions were not all myth. The older generation of Maa women scoff at the ways of their younger counterparts. She documents this disconnect through her lens using herself as a standard transcending cultural backgrounds while paying homage to a woman's true worth.

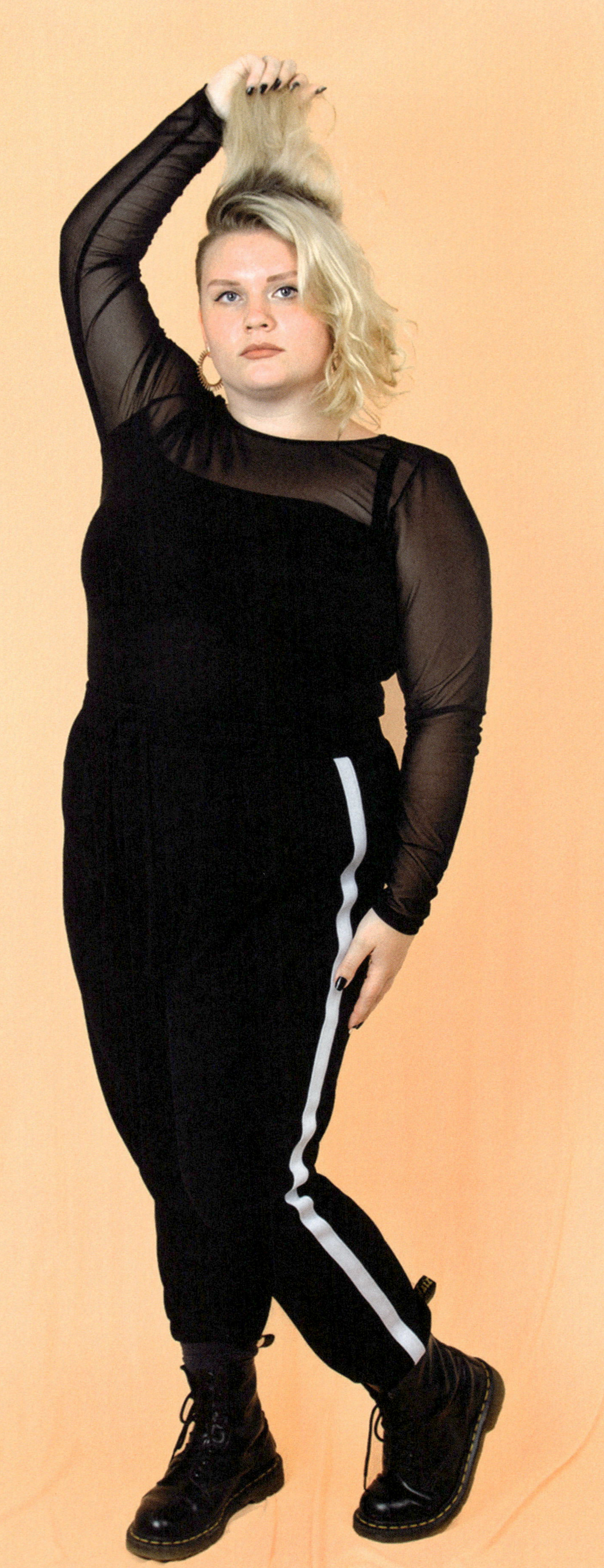

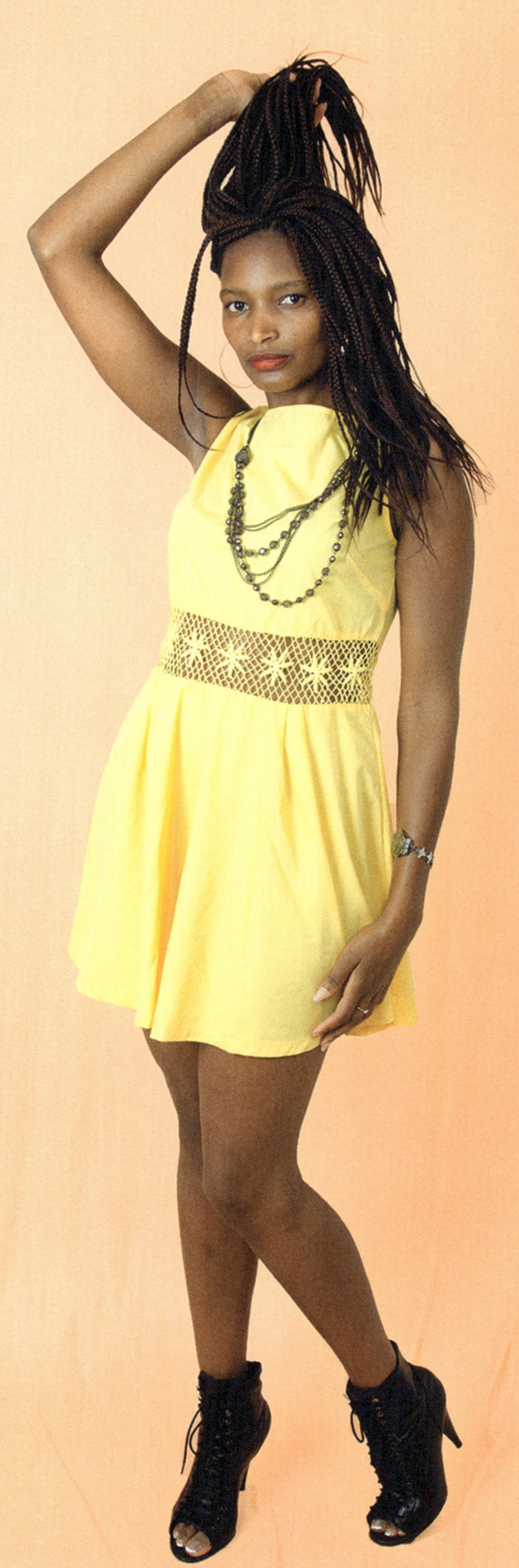

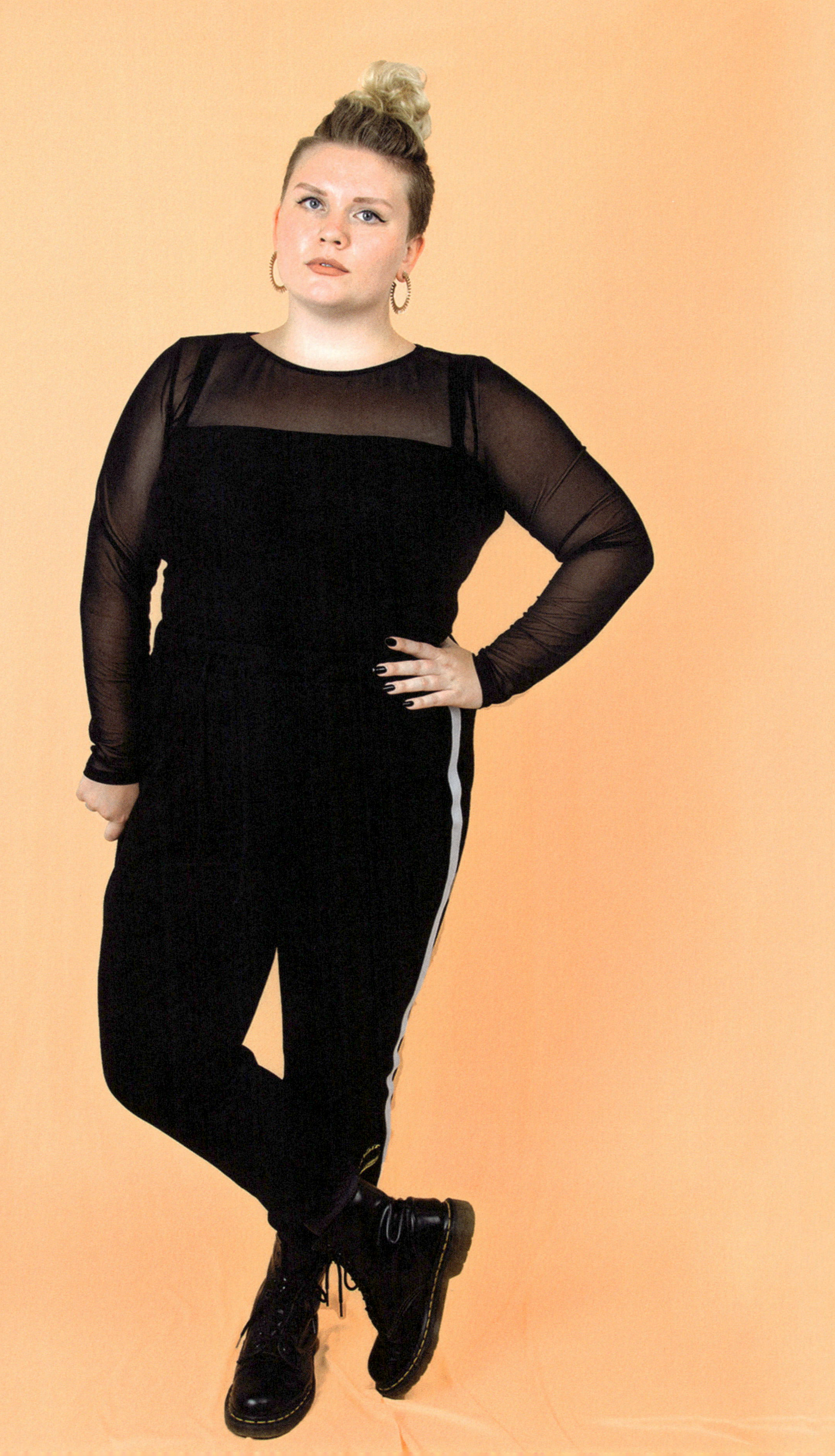

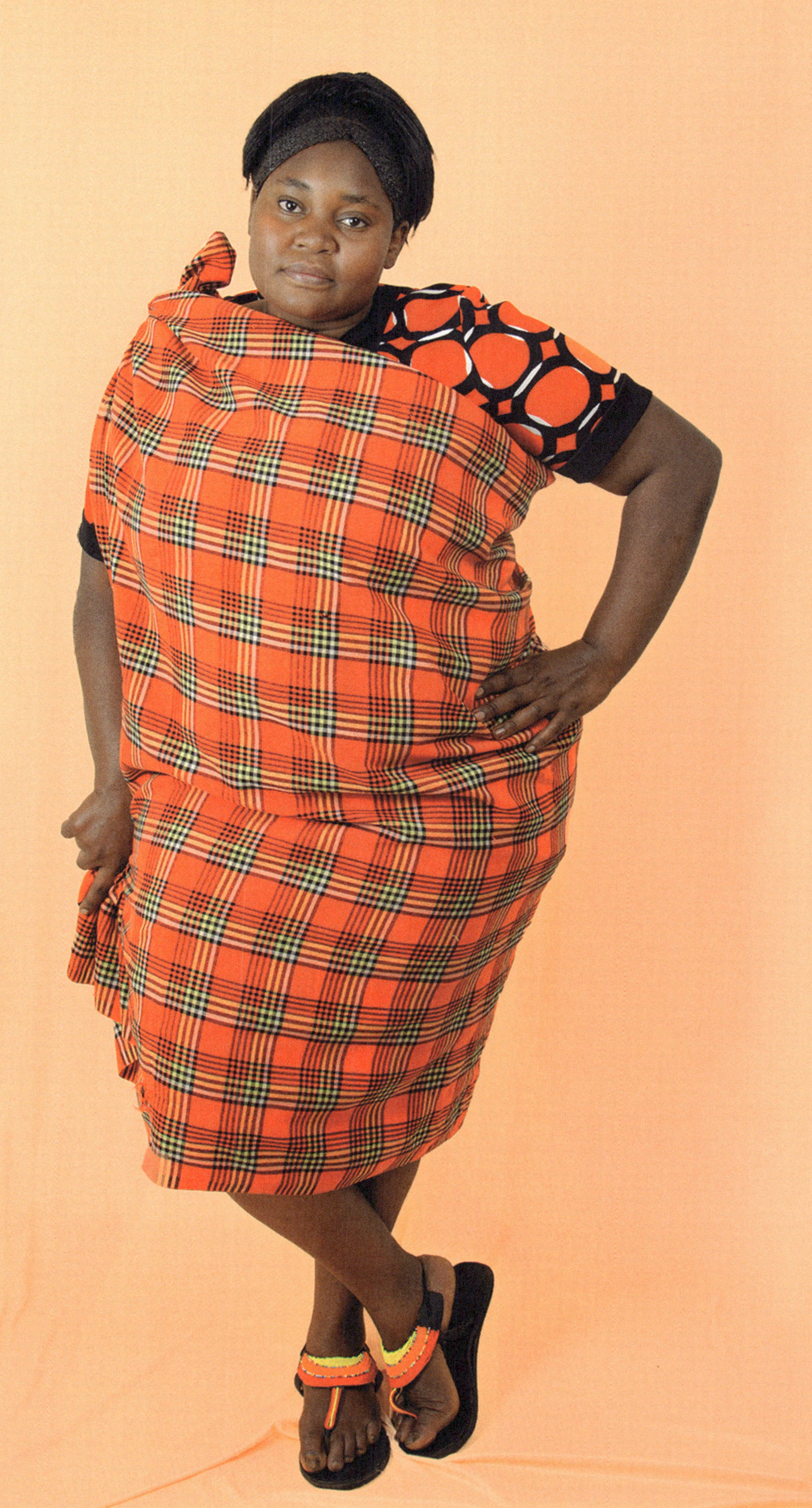

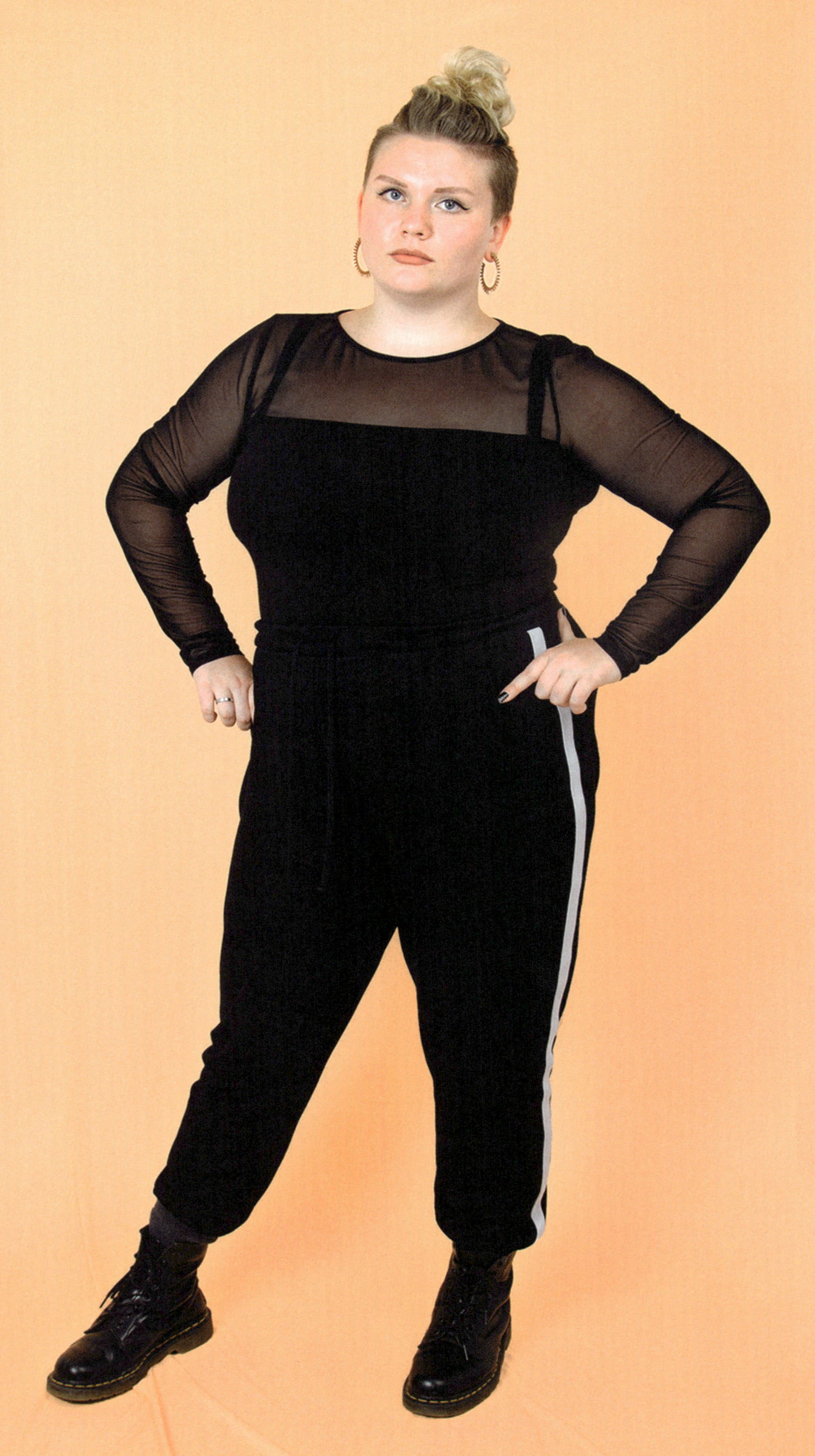

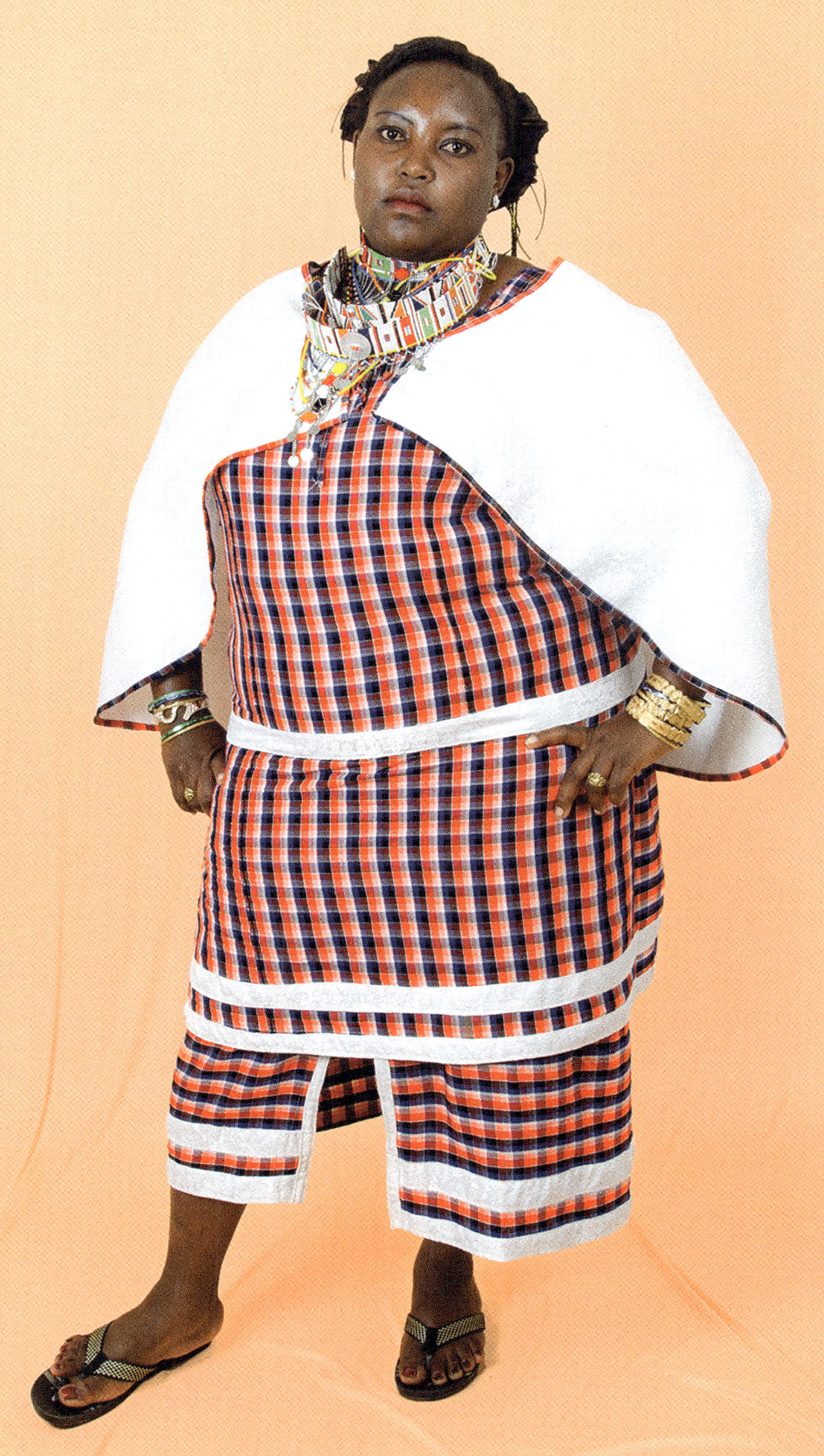

Kelvin Kiarie

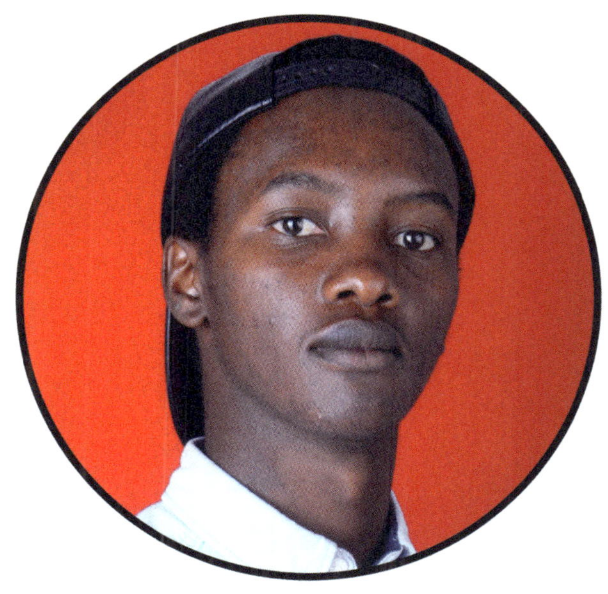

Grew up in: Nakuru and Nairobi

Age: 21

21-year-old Kelvin Kiarie is haunted by thoughts of a dystopian world overrun by Maasai vampires killing for human blood because their usual diet of raw cow blood with milk has lost all potency. By combining cleverly composed images with a chilling aesthetic, Kelvin tries to convey this absurd and irrational fear to his audiences. His work is testament to the boundlessness of his imagination which by allowing him such extents brings forth stunning visceral art.

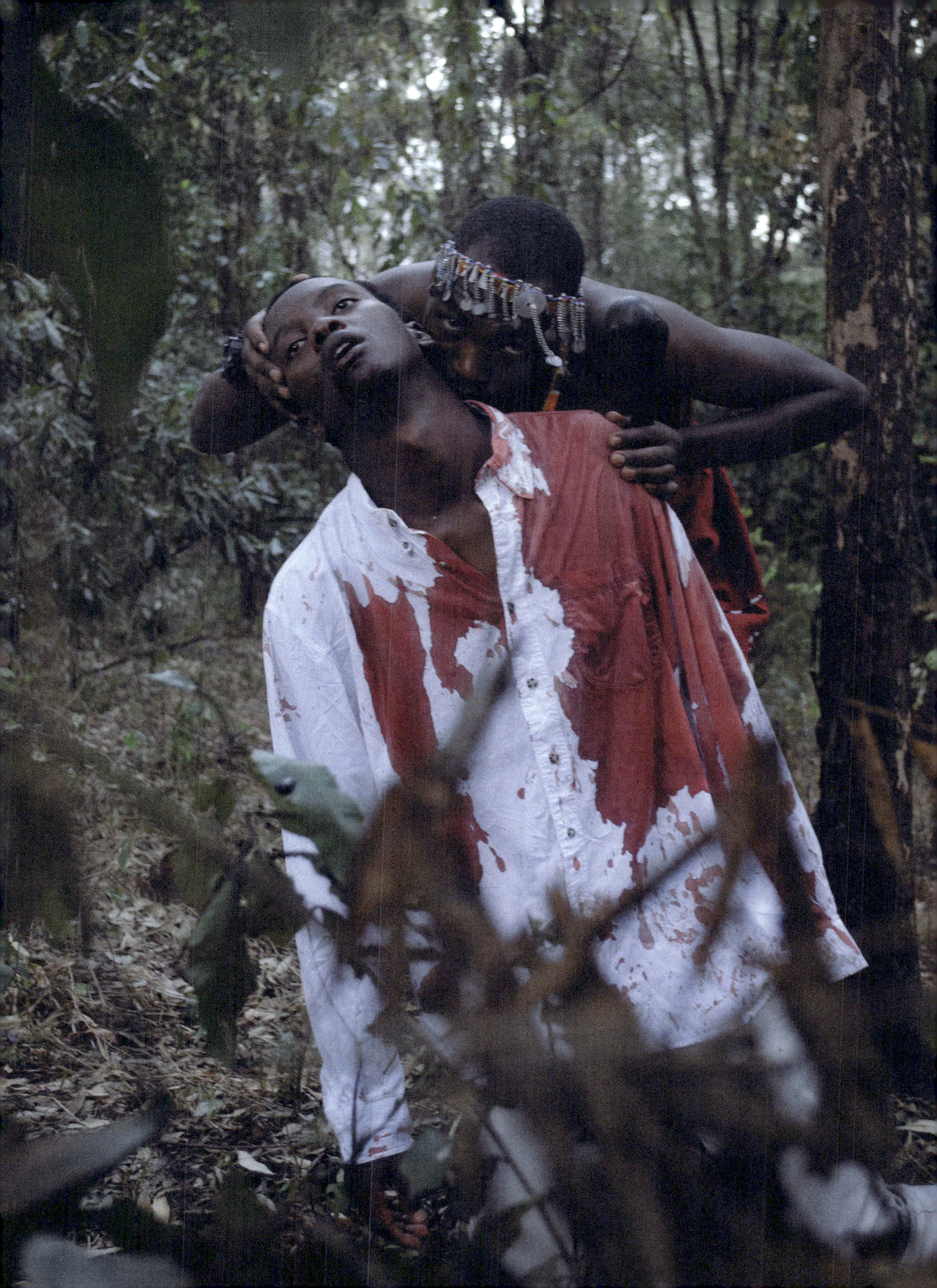

Waitherero Wambui

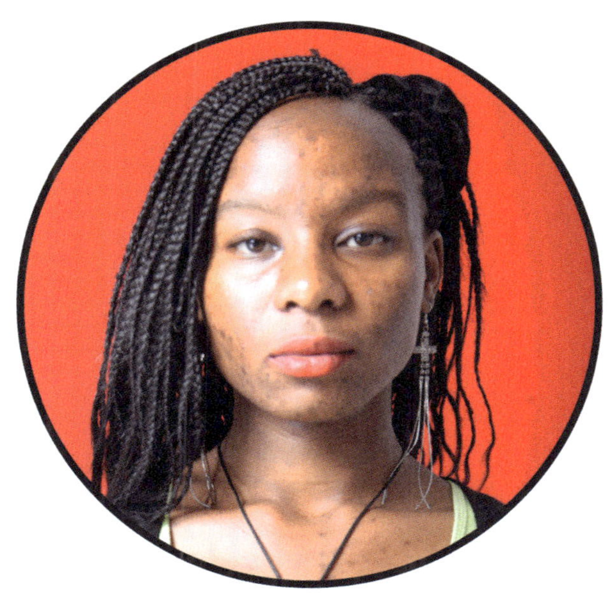

Grew up in: Nairobi
Age: 20

For a photographer nursing a secret to one day get into fashion styling, Maasai women are the perfect muses. Waitherero Wambui is one such artiste. The face of a Maa woman is for the young photographer reminiscent of many that she has seen walking the runways of high-end fashion shows or in glamour magazines; high cheek bones, angular jaw lines, intense eyes, bold stares. She combines contemporary edge inspired by her style icon Victoria Beckham with the vibrant colours of traditional Maa adornment to create an improbable hybrid which she calls 'Rock star Maasai'.

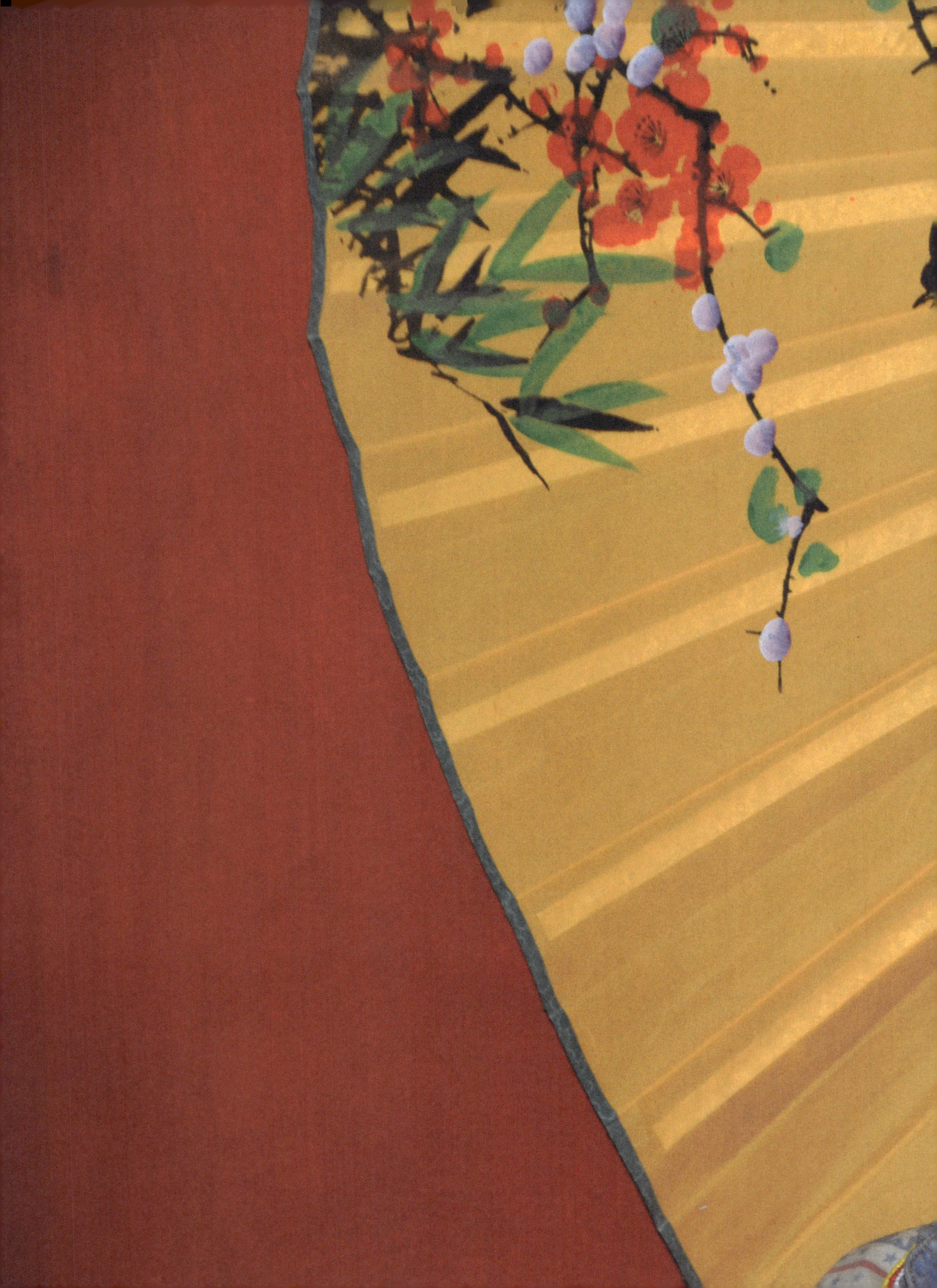

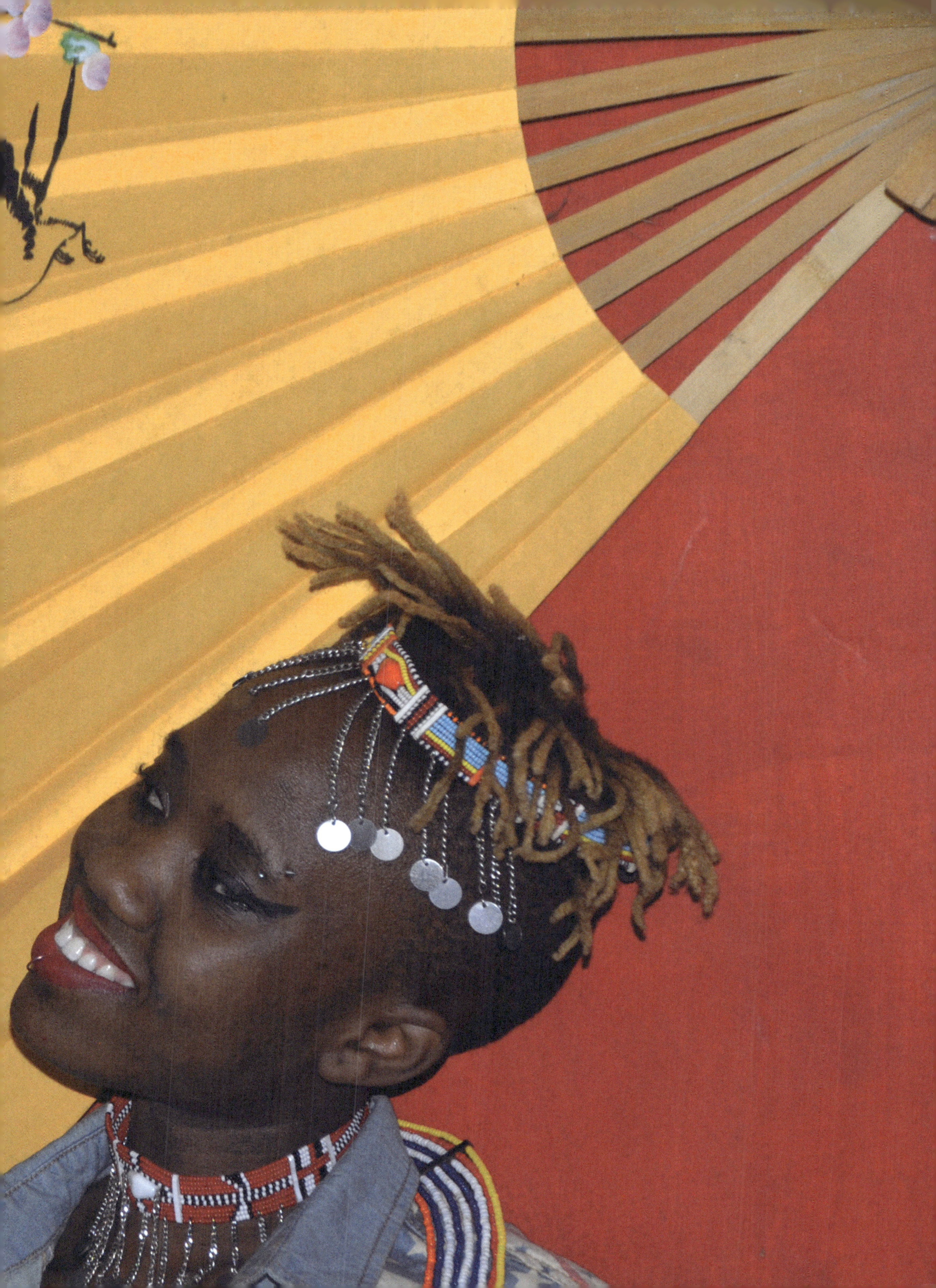

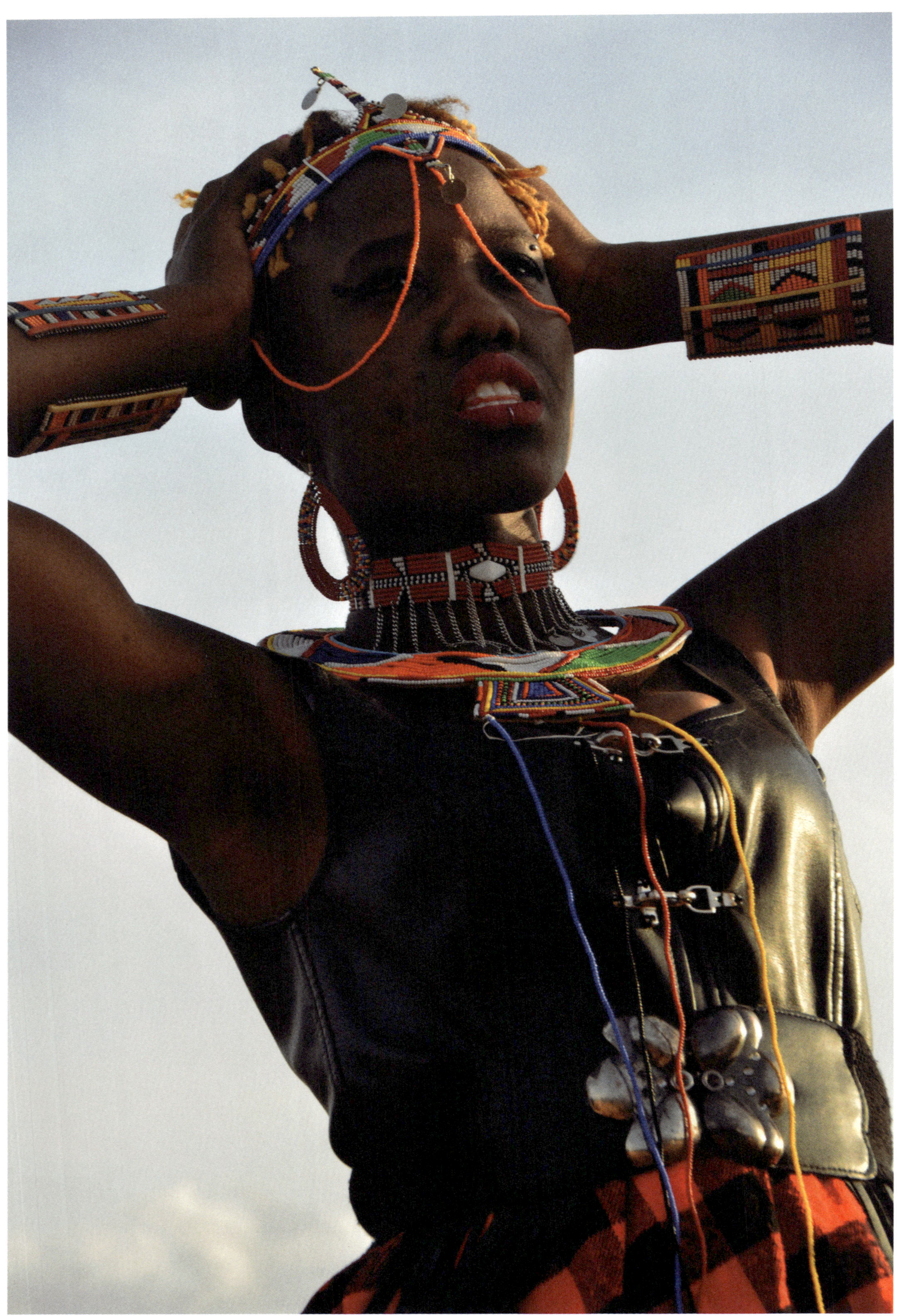